The Impact of the Sharing Economy on Business and Society

The emergence of new platform business models, notably the sharing economy, is impacting the economy in various ways, altering the structure of many industries, and raising a number of economic and political issues.

This book investigates the widespread influence of the sharing economy on businesses and society, as well as examining its underpinning economic principles and development. This volume presents an exhaustive review of the existing knowledge on the sharing economy and addresses several major areas of concern for incumbent businesses. It also explains the business models for those who are interested in embarking on their own ventures and provides an excellent source for further research. It takes an in-depth look at controversial labour policies, such as using labour as self-employed contractors or using regulatory grey areas to expand in markets. It is highly multidisciplinary, establishing links between economics, finance, marketing and consumer behaviour. This contribution on the sharing economy will enable researchers and graduate and doctoral students to expand and improve their understanding of this topic and identify new research problems in all of these areas.

The book will also appeal to policy makers, regional and local government decision makers, and those interested in labour markets transformation

Abbas Strømmen-Bakhtiar is Professor of Strategy and Technology at the Graduate School of Business, Nord University, Norway. His field of interest includes, but is not limited to, Digital Economy, Sharing Economy, Cloud Computing, Technology Management and Strategic Management. His most recent work is the book *Introduction to Digital Transformation and Its Impact on Society*.

Evgueni Vinogradov is a Senior Researcher at Nordland Research Institute, Bodo, Norway. He fields of interest include, among other areas, entrepreneurship and company establishment. He has broad experience from evaluations of business-oriented instruments and regional and industrial policy measures in Norway.

Routledge Studies in the Economics of Innovation

The Routledge Studies in the Economics of Innovation series is our home for comprehensive yet accessible texts on the current thinking in the field. These cutting-edge, upper-level scholarly studies and edited collections bring together robust theories from a wide range of individual disciplines and provide in-depth studies of existing and emerging approaches to innovation, and the implications of such for the global economy.

Automation, Innovation and Economic Crisis
Surviving the Fourth Industrial Revolution
Jon-Arild Johannessen

The Economic Philosophy of the Internet of Things
James Juniper

The Workplace of the Future
The Fourth Industrial Revolution, the Precariat and the Death of Hierarchies
Jon-Arild Johannessen

Economics of an Innovation System
Inside and Outside the Black Box
Tsutomu Harada

The Dynamics of Local Innovation Systems
Structures, Networks and Processes
Eva Panetti

Innovation in Knowledge Intensive Business Services
The Digital Era
Anna Cabigiosu

The Impact of the Sharing Economy on Business and Society
Digital Transformation and the Rise of Platform Businesses
Edited by Abbas Strømmen-Bakhtiar and Evgueni Vinogradov

For more information about this series, please visit: www.routledge.com/
Routledge-Studies-in-the-Economics-of-Innovation/book-series/ECONINN

The Impact of the Sharing Economy on Business and Society

Digital Transformation and the Rise of Platform Businesses

Abbas Strømmen-Bakhtiar and Evgueni Vinogradov

Routledge
Taylor & Francis Group

LONDON AND NEW YORK

First published 2020 by Routledge

2 Park Square, Milton Park, Abingdon, Oxon OX14 4RN
605 Third Avenue, New York, NY 10017

Routledge is an imprint of the Taylor & Francis Group, an informa business

First issued in paperback 2021

Publisher's Note

The publisher has gone to great lengths to ensure the quality of this reprint but points out that some imperfections in the original copies may be apparent.

British Library Cataloguing-in-Publication Data
A catalogue record for this book is available from the British Library

Library of Congress Cataloging-in-Publication Data
A catalog record has been requested for this book

ISBN: 978-0-367-26428-4 (hbk)
ISBN: 978-1-03-217602-4 (pbk)
DOI: 10.4324/9780429293207

Typeset in Bembo
by Swales & Willis, Exeter, Devon, UK

Dedicated to my wife Bente for her love and support
Abbas Strømmen-Bakhtiar

For my beloved wife Irina, who is so caring and supportive
Evgueni Vinogradov

List of Contributors

Anna Ilsøe, Employment Relations Research Centre, Department of Sociology, University of Copenhagen, Denmark

Trine Pernille Larsen, Employment Relations Research Centre, Department of Sociology, University of Copenhagen, Denmark

Christina Öberg, Örebro University, Sweden

Elena Dybtsyna, Nord University Business School, Norway

Terje Andreas Mathisen, Nord University Business School, Norway

Bjørn-Anders Carlsson, Nord University Business School, Norway

Kenneth Hardy, Nord University Business School, Norway

Abbas Strømmen-Bakhtiar, Nord University Business School, Norway

Evgueni Vinogradov, Nordland Research Institute, Norway

Birgit Leick, University of Southeastern Norway, Norway

Bjørnar Karlsen Kivedal, Høgskolen i Østfold, Norway

Mehtap Aldogan Eklund, University of Wisconsin-La Crosse, USA

Antonina Tsvetkova, Høgskolen i Molde, Norway

Contents

Preface

Access economy, peer economy, collaborative consumption, hippienomics, on demand economy, collaborative economy, gig economy, people economy, enabling economy, and empowering economy are some of the synonyms used for the often mentioned 'sharing economy'. But, 'sharing economy' is a misnomer, real sharing is one of the most important ingredients in the glue that holds societies together; hence, sharing has been with us for as long as human societies have existed. Indeed, we don't notice how our daily lives are full of small acts of sharing. In our homes, we share everything with our spouses and children except the toothbrush and some very personal items. We are also very generous towards our friends. They can borrow items, such as our tools, car, our cabin and other items. Then, it is our neighbours that can borrow items that they may need. Next, we have the constant sharing of roads, busses, schools, hospitals, parks and other public places. In addition, we freely give advice and inform others (sharing information), without expecting anything in return. In all these acts of sharing we seldom think about profit. Indeed, it is profit that changes the act of sharing into an economic exchange, rational and impersonal.

Throughout the ages, items such as rooms, horses, cars, construction equipment, and anything else of significant value were rented out for a price. The value of the object, the cost of finding a customer, finalising a contract and the ease of enforcing the said contract, determined the duration of the rental agreement and/or the price of service provided. There was also the critical issue of trust. In large physical markets, it is difficult to ascertain the trustworthiness of a stranger that one is entering into an economic transaction with. Only repeated dealings and proper enquiry can reduce the risk. The costs of all these activities or the "transaction costs" were high enough to influence the minimum rental period or the minimum cost of the services provided.

With the advent of the Internet and advances in communication, location, payment and Web technologies (Web 2.0), transaction costs were dramatically reduced, allowing for shorter contract time, and more innovative services. Many of the transactions are now provided by what is called a digital platform. Through these platforms, people can book flights, find taxis, book hotels, buy and sell shares and conduct a myriad of other economic transactions.

These platforms perform three key roles: provide an open, plug-and-play infrastructure, make available a secure transaction mechanism and provide a reputation system that many claim solves the problem of screening so that strangers can comfortably interact with each other. According to Simon (2011, Kindle Location 773) "the platform is becoming one of the most important business models of the new millennium – and with good reason. Buoyed by the success of Amazon, Apple, Facebook and Google, many exciting new companies are hitching their wagons on the platform" (see Figure 0.1).

We can say that the advent of the digital platform made the sharing economy possible. This is quite evident in the many definitions provided by organizations and scholars. For example, in their book *What's Mine Is Yours: The Rise of Collaborative Consumption*, Botsman and Rogers (2010, sec. Kindle locations 159–160) mix the traditional sharing with the rental/service platform business model. They define the collaborative consumption as "traditional sharing, bartering, lending, trading, renting, gifting and swapping, redefined through technology and peer communities".

A more precise definition is provided by the Department of Management and e-Government of the Norwegian Ministry of Local Government and Regional Development (CMD), which defines sharing economy as "Coupling between individuals and/or legal entities through digital platforms that facilitate the provision of services and/or sharing of assets/property, resources, expertise or capital without transferring ownership rights" ('Kartlegging av delingsøkonomien i Norge', 2016). In other words, sharing economy is a digital platform-based business model. These platforms have dramatically reduced the transaction costs, which in turn have opened the door to a world of innovations. This paper presents some of these innovations and their effects on the markets.

Chapter 1 explores the profitability of businesses using digital platforms. The results of the analysis demonstrate that the scope and size of income generated via digital platforms remains limited and online income is typically a supplement rather than the main income source. In addition, the findings also make a linkage between education, income and social status with the type of activities pursued on these platforms. For example, while highly educated persons with high incomes are active on capital platforms like Airbnb, the low-skilled workers, migrants, unemployed and young people are attracted to labour platforms such as Uber.

Chapter 2 examines three archetypes of financial sharing economy business models: the active investment in an idea; the banking clone and the hybrid. Activities, their linkages and who performs them vary with these archetypes, while the trustee and trust-facilitating activities also vary among them, making users, their ideas, or the platform the essential carrier of trust-establishing activities. The more trust, relying on the user, the more affective it is and the more limited is the spread of providers. This partially explains the success and failure of financial sharing economy operations.

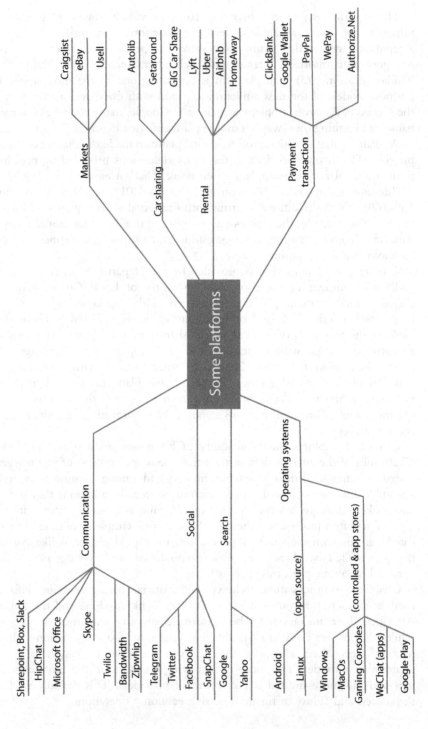

Figure 0.1 Some examples of platform models employed.

Chapter 3 examines the subject of Mobility as a Service (MaaS) as a new phenomenon of the sharing economy in transport services. The idea revolves around the meta-platform that integrates different platform solutions, like taxis, trains, buses, boats, ferries, and bike-sharing, into one platform. In such a meta-platform or alliance, trust, control and risk reduction are major issues that are examined and considered.

Chapter 4 looks at the effects of the increasing Airbnb activities on Norwegian house and rental prices. The adverse effects of Airbnb and other online marketplace and hospitality service brokerages on local rental conditions have been observed in many countries such as Germany, United Kingdom, Spain and others. This chapter concludes that if Airbnb expands at even half of its current rate of expansion, in a few years major Norwegian cities such as Oslo, Bergen, Trondheim and Tromsø will face a shortage of rental accommodation for their local populations.

Chapter 5 describes the sharing economy as a distinct type of digital entrepreneurship and gives first insights into its impact on regional economic development, which represents a hitherto unexplored topic. Using Airbnb rental data for the touristic destination of Østfold, a peripheral region of south-eastern Norway, this chapter describes digital entrepreneurship in the sharing economy as an alternative to traditional accommodation services and link its growth to regional employment and unemployment. Furthermore, the analysis indicates that the growth of these digital entrepreneurs in the region is driven by opportunity rather than necessity.

Chapter 6 looks into how the sharing economy has found its way into the offshore logistics operations in the ice-infested waters of the Barents Sea. This chapter shows how the sharing economy principles enable a number of value-creating activities in offshore logistics and create a shared value of collaborative resource utilization for local industries. It is further shown that some sharing economy principles can have trade-offs for allocation of transport resources in an optimal way to be able to respond quickly to any possible emergencies in hostile environments like the Arctic region.

Abbas Strømmen-Bakhtiar and Evgueni Vinogradov

1 Digital platforms at work

Champagne or cocktail of risks?

Anna Ilsøe and Trine Pernille Larsen

Introduction

Digital platforms such as Uber and Airbnb that facilitate the purchase and sale of services are an emerging phenomenon across the Western world and allow citizens to accrue income online. Since 2010, their effect on Western economies has attracted increasing academic and political attention (Collier et al. 2017). The debates emphasise, among other things, the implications of digital platforms for an individual's wage and working conditions (Wood et al. 2019) and national industrial relations (IR) models (Degryse 2017). Digital platforms are argued to change the employment relationship (De Groen and Maselli 2016), ease circumvention of labour standards (Goods et al. 2019), lead to unfair competition (Söderqvist 2017) and contribute to increased inequality (Schor 2016). Less researched are the potential linkages between distinct types of digital platform services and the levels of labour precariousness across and within Western economies.

This paper offers a novel perspective on the scope of digital platform economies and the dynamics between the institutional framework and the individual's exposure to precariousness when active on distinct digital platforms, even in densely regulated labour markets like Denmark. Denmark is well known for its universal welfare protection and strong IR-institutions that seemingly cushion individual's risks of in-work poverty, earnings inequalities and high job insecurities (Campbell and Price 2016). Thus, Denmark represents a critical case for examining the interlinkages between digital platforms and risks of precariousness, as institutions are in place to balance out potential labour market inequalities.

Our main research questions are: what is the scope of the digital platform economy; are distinct digital platforms associated with different levels of precariousness; and, if so, why. Our focal point is the individual's income generated via digital platforms and to what extent the low levels of protection on platforms are buffered by the wider institutional setting. The latter is defined here as employment and social protection provided to the individual through, for example, other jobs, the IR-system and the welfare state in terms of collectively agreed wages, statutory social assistance and unemployment benefits.

To address these questions, we draw on the first large-scale randomised survey on digital platforms in Denmark. Theoretically, we have sought inspiration from Thelen and Weidemann (2018). We infer that, although digital platforms have become more widespread, they are not necessarily accompanied by rising levels of precariousness, even if such online activities often operate outside the framework of most countries' labour laws and collective agreements. We argue that the risks of precariousness depend on how the wider institutional framework for social and employment protection, in combination with the individual, are able to mitigate the risks of operating in a non-regulated online market. In this context, we distinguish between two types of digital platforms: *labour platforms*, defined as digital intermediaries providing purchase and sale of typically labour-intensive services such as Uber; and *capital platforms*, which facilitate and provide rental of private property like Airbnb.

These two types of digital platforms are both expected to be associated with risks of precariousness, but at different levels due to the combined effects of a weak regulatory framework offering low levels of social protection and the differing characteristics of individuals accruing income from capital and labour platforms (Grimshaw et al. 2016; Rubery et al. 2018; Wood et al. 2019). Access to capital platforms is typically related to private ownership, whilst other dynamics like educational attainments and skill levels are assumed to apply to labour platforms (Healy et al. 2017). These differences are expected to influence individuals' exposure to precariousness, especially as their individual characteristics indicate their ability to compensate for the low levels of social and employment protection dominating capital and labour platforms.

This article is divided into five sections. First, we briefly discuss distinct forms of digital platforms. We then develop an analytical framework by reviewing the literature on digital labour, atypical and precarious employment. After this, the methods and data set used are presented, followed by our analysis. Finally, we discuss our findings.

Introducing the concepts of capital and labour platforms

There have been many concepts at play with regard to digital platforms. The European Commission (2016) has used the concept 'collaborative economy', whereas Danish unions prefer the concept of the 'platform economy' (LO 2016). A widely used concept is the 'sharing economy', which is often used in relation to distinct types of platforms where sharing, including exchange, rotation and fundraising take place (Schor 2016).

There is ample research that utilises various categories of digital platforms to capture the plethora of activities involved (Howcroft and Bregvall-Kåreborn 2019: 25). Such categories often include both narrow and wide definitions of digital platforms. Fuchs and Sevignani (2013) operate with one of the widest definitions, including paid and unpaid virtual work as well as users, providers and founders of digital platforms. We use a rather narrow definition and focus solely on the providers, i.e., those who accrue income through the digital platforms. We thereby omit the customers and founders, mainly because our aim is to gain insights into whether distinct digital platforms entail different exposure to risks of precariousness. Furthermore, we distinguish between two main types of digital platforms, while recognising that other studies operate with different categories and classifications.

The two main types of digital platforms used here are: 1) *capital platforms* that facilitate rentals of private property or belongings like Airbnb; and 2) *labour platforms* that facilitate the purchase and sale of typically labour intensive services like Uber (Farrell and Greig 2016; Schor and Attwood-Charles 2017). Other research also uses such categorisations, but tend to use them to illuminate common features associated with online activities rather than to explore the potential linkages between distinct platforms and the levels of precariousness, which is our paper's empirical focus (Howcroft and Bregvall-Kåreborn 2019: 25). The more specific characteristics of Danish labour and capital platforms are described in the analysis since the specifics of platforms typically vary depending on the national context including the regulations applicable to distinct platforms.

One of the challenges when investigating the size of income generated via digital platforms is to decide, which types of websites and apps fall within and outside these categories. With regard to labour platforms, we include platforms that facilitate work tasks – either as gigs (small tasks in the physical world) or as crowd work (small tasks done on the computer) (De Stefano 2016; Schmidt 2017). We have adopted a relatively narrow definition of capital platforms, which omits websites that facilitate buying and selling of used goods in our study. We are aware that this definition may result in our figures being more conservative compared to other studies like Farrell and Greig (2016). The reason for this choice is that we want to uncover whether and, if so how, digital platforms contribute to securing an ongoing income for individuals rather than an occasional sale of used belongings.

Digital platforms and risks of precariousness

Digital platforms are often considered to be yet another form of non-standard employment that exerts a downward pressure on wages, entails unfair competition and increases the risks of precarious employment in terms of poor job quality, lack of voice and high employment insecurities (Berg 2016; Goods et al. 2019). Such studies rarely distinguish between different digital platforms and their levels of precariousness and thus face similar criticism to much of the literature on atypical work. The latter research often overlooks the fact that a full-time permanent position is no guarantee against precariousness, whilst atypical work does not necessarily equal precariousness (Keune and Pedaci 2019: 2). However, strong links appear to exist between atypical work and precarious employment, although the risks of precariousness typically assume a different shape depending on the type of non-standard employment, where the welfare settlement and national IR-systems seem to play a part in cushioning the associated risks of precariousness (Campbell and Price 2016).

The dynamics between the institutional framework and the individual's exposure to precariousness when active on distinct digital platforms are less researched than other forms of non-standard employment (Schor and Attwood-Charles 2017). To encounter these shortcomings, we have sought inspiration from other streams of research on precarious and non-standard employment. Such studies typically emphasise different mechanisms fostering the recent rise in precarious employment (Emmenegger et al. 2012; Doellgast et al. 2018). They point, for example, to the changing landscape of industrial relations, with declining union densities, shrinking collective agreement coverage along with welfare retrenchment and labour market reforms that increasingly tie social benefits to employment status and collective agreements (Palier and Thelen 2010; Kalleberg and Vallas 2018: 5). The implications of these developments are argued to be a shift from collective mitigated risks by means of welfare and IR-settlements, towards increased individualised risks due to eroding employment and social protection (Kalleberg and Vallas 2018: 5). The regulatory setting with regard to digital platforms – especially labour platforms – is assumed to only fuel this development since digital platforms often redefine the traditional notion of employers and workers and facilitate solo self-employment. Thus, platforms abrogate the traditional employer responsibility of shouldering the costs of employee protection with resultant increased individualised risks of precariousness (Palier 2018). Much welfare and IR-literature stresses the pivotal role of the established system in striking new balances between flexibility and security to mitigate the gaps in protection emerging within the IR-settings and welfare arrangements following the growth in atypical work, including digital platforms (Grimshaw et al. 2016). To explore the scope of digital platforms and the potential linkages between distinct digital platforms and precariousness, we have sought inspiration from the work by Thelen (2019), Thelen and Weidemann (2018), although we only draw on selected aspects of their concepts. We choose this literature due to their notion that both the institutional framework for employment and social protection in combination with individual characteristics such as age, gender, ethnicity, educational attainment and employment prove critical to counteract or multiply precariousness. This will allow us to ascertain whether some digital platforms involve greater risks of precariousness than others, and how the institutional framework for social and employment protection in combination with the individual are able to mitigate the risks of operating in a less-regulated digital market.

Collective and individual risk protection

Thelen and Weidemann (2018) operate with two dimensions of risk – collective and individualised risk protection – and argue that they are pivotal to individuals' exposure to precariousness. *Collective risk protection* is concerned with how and to what degree established welfare and labour market institutions provide a safety net to mitigate risks of precariousness through social and employment protection. Here, we only consider employment and social protection provided by the IR-system and welfare state in terms of collective agreed minimum wages, statutory unemployment benefits and social assistance, while recognising that other forms of social protection like private insurances, health care etc., also buffer individuals from the low protection offered on digital platforms. *Individualised risk protection* is concerned with the individual's own resources and thus their ability to limit their risk exposure by securing other viable means of funding such as holding other jobs and having savings. The individual's characteristics such as age, ethnicity, gender, educational attainments and employment records prove pivotal to securing alternative avenues against precariousness (ibid.). Although collective and individualised risk protection are independent arrangements with different origins, they mutually reinforce one another by, in some instances, limiting or increasing individuals' exposure to precariousness depending on the institutional framework and the individual's characteristics. High levels of collective risk protection can compensate low levels of individualised risk protection and vice versa. However, the combined effects of low levels of collective and individualised risk protection may also increase risks of precariousness (ibid.). Therefore, risks of precariousness are expected to assume different forms across distinct types of non-standard employment, countries and institutional settings.

Applying the concepts of individualised and collective risk protection to our notion of two distinct digital platforms (i.e. labour and capital platforms), we expect that the activities taking place via these platforms will be associated with different levels of precariousness. Both the regulation of capital and labour platforms, including wage-setting and working conditions, is often left to market forces, since the traditional safety net of labour laws and collective agreements is limited, if not non-existent (Aleksynska et al. 2018). Therefore, digital platforms typically offer low levels of collective risk protection, leaving employment and social protection to be shouldered by the individual or the wider regulatory framework for social protection (Schor and Attwood-Charles 2017). We expect that the characteristics of individuals active on capital and labour platforms, and thus their level of individual risk protection, will differ, since distinct dynamics apply depending on the particular exchange of services.

Labour platforms entail that individuals in their capacity as labourers will accrue income by providing and selling their skills and services via the platform through various assignments. The possibility of offering small amounts of services in a highly flexible online setting may allow for new income opportunities for individuals with restricted working capabilities, or struggling entering the traditional job market (Healy et al. 2017). Therefore, we expect that low-skilled workers, women, migrants and young people will be overrepresented on labour platforms since studies on atypical work finds that these groups are particularly at risk of precariousness (Rubery et al. 2018). Such groups often work on the edges of the labour market or in less regulated sectors, where atypical work also tends to be widespread (Grimshaw et al. 2016).

Capital platforms operate in a different way, where income arises from commodifying private property exchanges by leasing private cars, houses or apartments via the platform. Thus, access to capital platforms seems implicitly conditioned by individuals' holding properties – rentals or acquired private property – to lease via the platform. The ability to acquire and then lease private property requires a relatively secure source of income gained through stable employment or by other viable means. Therefore, individuals active on capital platforms may hold stronger positions within the traditional labour market than their peers on labour platforms, where low entry barriers may ease integration of marginalised groups into the labour market (Healy et al. 2017).

The assumed differences in the characteristics of individuals active on capital and labour platforms are expected to influence their exposure to precariousness. We posit that low levels of precariousness will be found on capital platforms: individuals engaged in such online activities will, in their capacity as property owners and/or (often) secure employees in the traditional labour market, have other means to compensate for the weak regulatory framework characterizing capital platforms. Their high level of individual risk protection is expected to shelter them against the online risks of precariousness. The wider institutional framework for employment and social protection may also add another layer of protection, particularly if the capital platform providers combine their online activities with jobs in the traditional labour market. In such instances, online income is mainly a top-up for existing income sources and can be considered a pleasant, but unnecessary luxury like champagne.

The situation is expected to be somewhat different on labour platforms, where risks of precariousness are assumed to be more common due to the combined effects of the individual characteristics of platform workers and the weak regulatory framework for wage and working conditions. Their low levels of individual risk protection may only increase their risks of precariousness, especially if the wider regulatory setting for employment and social protection also fails to compensate for the gaps in protection on digital platforms. Therefore, labour platforms may involve a cocktail of risks, whilst the implications seem less severe on capital platforms due to individual's ability to compensate for the lack of social protection characterizing platforms through other viable means.

The developed analytical framework is used to study the scope of digital platforms and individuals' exposure to precariousness on distinct platforms. Such an analysis may also contribute to the further development of the models by Thelen and Weidemann (2018) into analytical tools when applying those models to forms of non-standard employment other than those for which their models were initially developed.

Methods and used data

To examine the scope of digital platforms, including the potential ties between distinct online activities and individuals' risks of precariousness, we draw on a large-scale survey involving 18,000 randomly selected Danish citizens aged 15–74 years, conducted as part of the Danish Labour Force Survey 2017. We thereby offer a novel cross-sectoral platform perspective in an emerging field, where most research either tends to focus on certain sectors or single case studies (Howcroft and Bregvall-Kåreborn 2019).

The Danish Labour Force Survey is conducted quarterly by Statistics Denmark and is based on a random sample of the population,[1] who are interviewed, using a combination of web survey and phone interviews. The quality and size of the Danish Labour Force Survey gives us access to solid figures on the scope of digital platforms, which are a growing, but still limited, phenomenon. The standard survey also includes many relevant questions on demographics to which we added three questions on digital platforms. We asked the respondents, if they had accrued income by performing tasks found via digital platforms during the last 12 months. We also asked, if they had had income by leasing their property via digital platforms during the past 12 months. The third question addressed the level of income generated via digital platforms. Prior to data collection, we conducted a pilot test and adjusted the wording of the questions. The survey was conducted during the first quarter of 2017 and received responses from 18,043 Danes, corresponding to a response rate of 54 percent.

The data generated as part of the Danish Labour Force Survey was used to examine the potential linkages between distinct types of digital platforms and risks of precariousness, using descriptive statistics and regression analysis. We used the following dependent and independent variables in our analysis.

- *Dependent variables*: income via labour platforms, income via capital platforms, total income from platforms.
- *Independent variables*[2]: gender, age, ethnicity, education, employment status, total income of employed citizens.

Our analytical strategy was twofold: Firstly, we examined how digital platforms are regulated in Denmark (based on desk research) and mapped the share of Danes with incomes from the two types of digital platforms, along with the related income levels from such sources (descriptive statistics). Secondly, we examined the profile of platform providers (their labour market status, demographic characteristics) and thus sought to answer our main research question of whether distinct digital platforms involve greater risks of precariousness than others (regression analysis). The latter analysis includes two binary regressions (using linear probability models): one examining the correlation between an individual's likelihood of accruing income via a labour platform and their individual characteristics; and a second regression analysis on the characteristics of people who have accrued income via a capital platform.

Analysis

Digital platforms and the Danish labour market

The first digital platforms arrived in Denmark in the 2000s. The first capital platform was a Danish-owned car-pooling service (GoMore), which was launched in 2005 and later developed into a site for private car rentals. Labour platforms came a few years after the first capital platforms. Uber launched its Uber Pop service in Denmark in 2014, but ceased their services again in April 2017. Throughout 2015 and 2016 different Danish-owned labour platforms emerged, especially within the field of cleaning (for instance Happy Helper and Hilfr). There has been considerable debate in the media and among Danish politicians and social partners, as to how to perceive and regulate digital platforms. Recent court rulings have contributed to clarifying matters.

Capital platforms are by definition not part of the labour market, as income from rentals through platforms is considered to be a capital return according to Danish law (Ilsøe and Madsen 2018). Nevertheless, income via capital platforms may still affect individual's behaviour, not least regarding risks of precariousness since activity on a capital platform, in principle, is related to private ownership. Debates on capital platforms have centered on the lack of tax payments on income accrued via the platforms, and Danish tax authorities, among others, have produced a number of guidelines on how to correctly report private income via capital platforms.[3] In Spring 2018, the Danish government signed an agreement with Airbnb that granted higher thresholds for tax-free income via the platform on condition that all income accrued via the Airbnb platform is automatically reported to the Danish tax authorities. However, the agreement has not been implemented yet.

Labour platforms are considered as part of the Danish labour market. Therefore, income generated via labour platforms is subject to income taxation. Labour platforms typically operate by allowing larger or smaller bids of particular tasks to be performed by individuals who are not employed by the platform, and thus not considered to be workers or employees. Instead, they are perceived as self-employed or independent contractors that provide services facilitated through and by the platform. Individuals active on labour platforms are legally obliged to register with the Danish VAT register and pay VAT, if their income via the platforms reaches a certain threshold (€6,666 per year).

Both capital and labour platforms operate in a less-regulated online setting, where market forces regulate pricing and working conditions (Ilsøe and Madsen 2017). The notion of individuals selling their services via digital platforms being self-employed leaves them with limited, if any coverage from Danish collective agreements and labour laws. However, Danish social partners have, with varying success, attempted to cover individuals on platforms, especially those operating on the labour platforms.[4] Nonetheless, most individuals engaged in online activities operate outside the range of the Danish IR-model. This leaves most platform workers in a protective gap with lower levels of collective risk protection than employees covered by collective agreements or Danish labour laws (Ilsøe and Madsen 2018). They often share these conditions with other forms of non-standard workers on the Danish labour market (freelancers, temporary employed and marginal part-timers etc.), who also tend to have less coverage from Danish laws and collective agreements (Larsen 2011; Scheuer 2017).

The Danish labour market is characterised by wage and working conditions being primarily regulated through collective agreements signed by social partners at sectoral and company levels (Larsen et al. 2010). Legislation plays a more limited role – primarily in areas like gender equality, health and safety, holiday entitlements, vocational and further training (Due and Madsen 2008). This institutional set-up cushions, to some extent, the effects of the unregulated digital platforms. An example of how the Danish IR-model limits the effects is the collective agreed wages' positive knock-on effects on wage-setting in the unorganised parts of the labour market, including digital labour platforms (Larsen 2011). Digital cleaning platforms like Happy Helper[5] and Hilfr[6] offer an hourly price ranging from €15.70 to €16.60 to their service suppliers, which nearly resembles the minimum collective agreed wage (€17) within the Danish cleaning sector (DI 2017). However, while such platform workers may receive nearly the same minimum hourly payment as their peers covered by collective agreements, their hourly payment is considerably lower than the average hourly wages (€22.30) within the cleaning sector due to their limited access to wage supplements (Ilsøe et al. 2017). Furthermore, with the exception of Hilfr, they also have no rights to other collectively agreed benefits like pensions, further training, paid sick leave or maternity leave and are thus expected to shoulder such costs individually without being compensated through higher hourly payments (Ilsøe and Madsen 2018). Therefore, the Danish IR-model appears unable to compensate for most protection gaps on digital platforms, leaving it to the Danish welfare state or individuals themselves to provide a safety net when active in the digital labour market.

The Danish welfare state provides, with its universal citizenship-based welfare services, limited usage of means-testing and employment-related benefits – a safety net for those operating on the edges of the labour market (Esping-Andersen 1999). However, shifting Danish governments have gradually tied social protection to employment status and collective agreement coverage (Larsen and Mailand 2018). This adds to the pressure on platform workers with regard to social protection: they often struggle to meet the tighter eligibility criteria for unemployment benefit and social assistance. They thus experience lower levels of collective risk protection as most welfare institutions are founded on the assumption of employees' holding permanent full-time positions or working full time on a self-employed basis. On the other hand, the Danish social assistance and unemployment benefit schemes may prevent a race to the bottom on the platforms: they implicitly provide a wage floor, which is difficult for the platforms to ignore, if they want to attract individuals to sell their services. The lowest level of monthly unemployment benefits range from €1,665 for part-time insured workers to €2,457 for full-time insured workers. Moreover, monthly levels of social assistance range from €972 to €2,000 depending on age and provider roles (Mailand and Larsen 2018). Therefore, Danish social protection may also limit a downward spiral on wage and working conditions on digital platforms.

Digital platforms, their scope and size of generated income

The digital platforms operating in Denmark involve only a small fraction of the workforce. Our survey results indicate that 2.4 percent of Danes had purchased and sold services via either a digital labour or a capital platform during the last year. Around 1.4 percent – had accumulated income by leasing their private properties via a capital platform, whilst 1 percent of Danes reported income arising from labour platforms. Thus, Danes seem more likely to use capital platforms than labour platforms to top up their income (Table 1.1). These results are in line with a number British and American quantitative studies (Farrell and Greig 2016; Katz and Krueger 2016; Rubery et al. 2018)

Activity on one type of platform is rarely related to activity on other types of platforms. Less than 0.1 percent have been active on both types of platforms within the last year. Therefore, most individuals involved in such online activities often generate income exclusively from capital platforms (1.4 percent of Danes) or labour platforms (0.9 percent of Danes), respectively (Table 1.1).

The level of income accrued via digital platforms is relatively modest on both labour and capital digital platforms. For example, 61 percent of Danes generating income via a labour platform within the last 12 months had earned less than €3,330 annually before taxes whilst 71 percent of Danes providing services via a capital platform had generated less than €3,330 annually before taxes within the last year (Table 1.2).

Table 1.1 The share of Danes aged 15–74 accruing income via digital capital and/or labour platforms during the past 12 months in percent

	Accrued income solely via labour platform	Accrued income solely via a capital platform	Accrued income via both capital and labour platforms	Total share of population accruing income from capital or labour platforms
Yes	0.9	1.4	0,1*	2.4
No	99.1	98.6	99.9	97.6
Total	100	100	100	100

Source: authors' own calculations based on weighted data, * unreliable estimate due to small N.

Table 1.2 How much money have you accrued via websites or apps over the past
12 months – before taxes? (In percent of all who reported an income via
a labour of capital platform, respectively)

	Labour platforms	Capital platforms
Less than DKK 25.000 (€3.330)	61	71
DKK 25.000 (€ 3.330) or more	12	19
Don't know	28	9*
Total	100	100

Source: authors' own calculations based on a weighted data, * unreliable estimate due to
small N.

The modest level of income generated via a capital and/or labour platform
indicates potential risks of precariousness. Furthermore, the division between
individuals active on labour platforms and capital platforms calls for further
investigation – especially with regard to their demographics, labour market
status and educational attainment as these factors are assumed to influence
such individuals' level of risk protection and thus exposure to precariousness
(Rubery 2015).

Labour platforms and individuals' exposure to risk of precariousness

Less than 1 percent of Danes have sold services via a labour platform, and few of
these – 12 percent – generated more than €3,330 within the last year. A large
minority group – 28 percent – were unable to report on their annual income generated via a labour platform (Table 1.2). This indicates that unless such platform
workers combine their income via the labour platform with other income sources,
they face increased risks of precariousness, particularly considering the Danish
living costs. In this context, our regression results demonstrate that labour market
status and a number of demographic variables correspond closely with whether or
not individuals offer and sell their services via a labour platform (Table 1.3).

Labour market status appears to influence the activity levels on labour platforms. Unemployed workers seem more likely than others to generate income
via a labour platform, followed by retirees, students and other people outside the
labour force.[7] In fact, employed people are less likely than others to do so (Table
1.3). When looking at employed citizens active on the platforms, we find an
over representation of those with lower earnings. Thirty-two per cent of these
are located in the two lowest income deciles of adult Danes. Further analyses also
indicate a close link between employment contracts, earnings and activity levels
on labour platforms. Fixed-term and temporary agency workers are more active
on labour platforms than employees with other employment contracts. Likewise,
we find an overrepresentation of employees with low tenure (less than three
years) on the labour platforms. These results suggest that labour platforms, in line

Table 1.3 Linear probability regression model: probability of income on capital and labour forms depending individual characteristics

	Labour platforms		Capital platforms	
	Base model	Full-model	Base model	Full-model
Male (ref)	0.00	0.00	0.00	0.00
	(.)	(.)	(.)	(.)
Female	−0.04***	−0.08***	0.02***	0.07***
	(0.00)	(0.00)	(0.00)	(0.00)
15–19 years (ref)		0.00		0.00
		(.)		(.)
20–29 years		−0.29***		0.33***
		(0.01)		(0.01)
30–39 years		−0.40***		0.43***
		(0.01)		(0.01)
40–49 years		−0.28***		0.34***
		(0.01)		(0.01)
50–59 years		−0.51***		0.50***
		(0.01)		(0.01)
60–74 years		−0.64***		0.65***
		(0.01)		(0.01)
Danish (ref)		0.00		0.00
		(.)		(.)
Other ethnic backgrounds		0.10***		−0.10***
		(0.00)		(0.00)
Primary education (ref)		0.00		0.00
		(.)		(.)
Upper secondary & vocational training		0.17***		−0.16***
		(0.01)		(0.00)
Higher education (short)		−0.06***		0.07***
		(0.01)		(0.01)
BA		−0.02***		0.07***
		(0.01)		(0.01)
MA & PhD		−0.09***		0.10***
		(0.01)		(0.01)

(Continued)

Table 1.3 (Cont.)

	Labour platforms		Capital platforms	
	Base model	Full-model	Base model	Full-model
Employed (ref)		0.00 (.)		0.00 (.)
Unemployed		0.26*** (0.01)		−0.24*** (0.01)
Retirees etc.		0.17*** (0.00)		−0.16*** (0.00)
Constant		0.72*** (0.01)	0.70*** (0.00)	0.28*** (0.01)
N (weighted data)		97,787	97,787	97,787
r2		0.19	0.00	0.19

Linear probability model
Standard errors in parentheses
*$p < 0.05$
**$p < 0.01$
***$p < 0.001$

with our expectations, especially attract groups with low individual risk protection in that they are more likely to be at the margins of the Danish labour market. Such groups rarely have alternative resources at their disposal to limit their exposure to precariousness and are thus unable to compensate for the weak regulatory framework characterising labour platforms. Their low levels of individual risk protection seem even more apparent when controlling for other factors such as age, gender, ethnicity and educational attainment (Table 1.3).

Activities on labour platforms seem to be age related: young people aged 15–19 years are more likely to offer and sell services via a labour platform than their older peers. However, the effect of age diminishes somewhat when controlling for other factors (Table 1.3). Our regression results also indicate that men are more likely than women to accrue income via labour platforms. The same applies to low-skilled workers, whilst those with higher education (short, BA or MA/PhD) are least likely to do so. Moreover, people with ethnic backgrounds other than Danish are more likely to be active on labour platforms (Table 1.3). These findings contribute to a picture where many platform workers seem to have limited individual means to counteract their exposure to low income on digital platforms and thus risks of precariousness: they are more likely to be low skilled with scarce financial resources. In fact, the combined effects of their individual characteristics seem to reflect a cocktail of risks, where the wider institutional framework offer some collective risk protection. Many platform workers in their capacity as unemployed workers, retirees, students or social assistance claimants receive unemployment benefits, student allowances or social assistance, which they often appear to combine with income accrued via labour platforms. Thereby, Danish social protection schemes seem to compensate for the low levels of individual risk protection and weak regulatory framework dominating Danish labour platforms.

Capital platforms and individuals' exposure to risk of precariousness

Around 1.4 percent of Danes had generated income via a capital platform within the last year and, among those, 71 percent had earned less than DKK 25,000 (€3,330) while 19 percent reported higher financial returns from the capital platform. Around 10 percent were unable to report on their annual income generated via a capital platform (Table 1.2). The reported income levels via capital platforms appear modest and thus capital platforms seem to entail similar exposure to risks of precariousness as the labour platforms insofar as the individuals active on capital platforms are unable to top up their income via the capital platform with other sources of income. Our regression analysis of who accumulates income via capital platforms demonstrates a close interaction with labour market status and demographic characteristics, although with very different results compared to the individuals active on labour platforms (Table 1.3).

Among capital platform providers, the oldest segments (50–59 years, 60–74 years) are most likely to generate income via capital platforms, whereas youngest people aged 15–19 years are least likely to lease their properties via a capital platform. Focusing on labour market status, employed people are most likely to accumulate income via a capital platform. Retirees, students and other people outside the labour force come in second, whereas unemployed people are least active on capital platforms when measured in terms of financial returns. It seems that individuals active on capital platforms often have an older age profile than their peers on labour platforms as well as they are more often employed. Further analysis indicates that they often hold open-ended contracts. This is perhaps not surprising, as many tend to settle in the labour market with a stable or increasing income, as they grow older. Such stability allows people to purchase their own home, car, and other belongings, which they afterwards can lease via capital platforms. Combining our analysis with income data, we find that 30 percent of employed providers of services on capital platforms have a total income in the top two income deciles of the Danish adult population. Thus, Danes with a higher total income seem overrepresented on capital platforms, whilst we saw the opposite among individuals active on labour platforms.

Such results imply, in line with our expectations, that capital platforms attract very different groups from labour platforms in that the former is more likely than the latter to have a stronger foothold in the traditional labour market and to have other means of income at their disposal. They thus have higher levels of individual risk protection that shelter them against the unregulated online market and its associated risks. The high levels of individual risk protection among individuals active on capital platforms are further underlined when controlling for other factors such as gender, ethnicity and educational attainment (Table 1.3).

In contrast to the labour platforms, women are more likely than men to accumulate income via capital platforms. Education and ethnicity also play a role, but in a different way from the patterns found among providers on labour platforms: people with higher education (BA or MA/PhD) are more likely to generate income via capital platforms compared to their peers with lower levels of educational attainments. Moreover, and in sharp contrast to our findings regarding individuals on labour platforms, we also find that ethnic Danes are overrepresented on capital platforms (Table 1.3).

These results imply, in line with our expectations, that the combined effects of the individual characteristics of people active on capital platforms reduce their exposure to precariousness in that their high-skill levels, combined with stable employment and substantial savings, provide them with a safety net that compensates for the gaps in protection dominating the online market. The Danish welfare state and IR-model seem to only strengthen or multiply their risk protection since they add another layer of social and employment protection for most individuals, especially those that combine their online activities with jobs in the organised labour market. This also indicates that risks of precariousness seem less common on capital platforms, but only because individuals, in combination with the social protection offered by the wider institutional framework, are able to compensate for the weak regulatory framework of capital platforms. Therefore, online income resembles a pleasant, but unnecessary luxury, like champagne.

Discussion and conclusion

Citizens of the Western world increasingly seek supplementary income online – either by leasing their property or by taking on extra assignments via a digital platform. This has given rise to academic and political debates on how to conceptualise and regulate such online activities, including their implications for an individual's exposure to precariousness when active on distinct platforms like labour and capital platforms. Three main aspects are emphasised in the discussion of our findings.

Firstly, our analysis demonstrates that income accrued via digital platforms is rather modest in Denmark with 2.4 percent of Danes providing and selling their services via online apps or websites. In most cases such sources of online income represent a supplement rather than the main source of income for individuals active on digital platforms, findings that echo other European and American studies (Katz and Krueger 2016; Rubery et al. 2018). However, among the 2.4 percent of individuals actively providing and selling services via a digital platform, marked differences can be traced between those active on a labour platform and their peers on capital platforms. It is rarely the same people selling their labour and renting out their private properties via digital platforms. Less than 0.1 percent of Danes have been active on both types of platforms within the last year and further analyses indicate, in line with our expectations, that the characteristics of the individuals active on labour platforms and capital platforms differ considerably when comparing their demographics, labour market status, level of educational attainment and overall income levels. In fact, certain groups such as young people, low-skilled, low paid and unemployed people, temporary employees and non-ethnic Danish were more likely to accrue income via labour platforms; whilst their older and often higher educated and more well-off peers with stronger labour market ties (they were employed) tended to be overrepresented among capital platform providers. Our results echo other American and European studies, which also suggest that it is rarely the same people selling their labour and leasing their private properties/possessions via websites and apps (Farrell and Greig 2016; Katz and Krueger 2016). The fact that labour platforms seem to attract low-skilled workers, young people, unemployed and low-income groups points to their limited means to purchase private property which can then be leased via a capital platform. This also seems to explain the limited overlap between individuals accruing income via digital labour and capital platforms as well as their level of exposure to precariousness when active online.

Secondly, our findings support our notion that capital and labour platforms are associated with different levels of precariousness, even if both platforms represent less or non-regulated online settings. The differences in the characteristics of individuals accruing income via labour and capital platforms put individuals on labour platforms at greater risks of precariousness than their peers on capital platforms due to their lower levels of individual risk protection. Therefore, individuals renting their properties via capital platforms seem in a better position than individuals on labour platforms to mitigate the effects arising from the weak regulatory framework and thus to limit their exposure to precariousness. Their higher skill levels combined with stable employment and substantial savings provide them with a safety net that compensates for the gaps in protection dominating the online market. The Danish welfare state and IR-model seem to strengthen capital platform providers' risk protection since the wider institutional framework adds another layer of social and employment protection especially for those that combine their online activities with jobs in the organised labour market. The situation is somewhat different for most groups active on labour platforms, even if the Danish welfare state and IR-model also – to some extent – shoulder their risks of low levels of social protection on the labour platforms. In fact, labour platforms appear to especially attract groups that seek to gain a foothold in the Danish labour market. Unemployed people and young people at the start of their career are more likely to generate income via labour platforms than other platform providers. Likewise, non-ethnic Danes were overrepresented – a group that generally find it difficult entering the Danish labour market (Ejrnæs 2006). This indicates – in line with our expectations – that labour platforms, on the one hand, may contribute to increased risks of precariousness due to the combined effects of a rather unregulated setting and individuals with low levels of individual risk protection. However, on the other hand, labour platforms may also foster labour market inclusion for groups often struggling to gain employment.

Thirdly, with regard to the wider institutional framework and its pivotal role in mitigating the effects of low levels of social and employment protection on digital platforms, the Danish welfare state and IR-model seem to make a difference, but in distinct ways. Our analysis points to the fact that people using capital platforms are of less risk of precariousness than those using labour platforms. The recent government led reforms that tighten the eligibility criteria for unemployment benefits and social assistance seem to place additional pressure on some digital platform providers (Mailand and Larsen 2018). Their low income generated via digital platforms suggest few contracted hours and especially those with no other jobs may struggle to qualify for unemployment benefits and social assistance as these schemes are earnings-related or depend on past employment records, including the number of hours worked while in employment (Larsen and Mailand 2018). Therefore, the established institutional framework seems in some instances to contribute to the cocktail of risks for some digital platform providers, especially those selling their services via labour platforms. The policy implications thus far have been a reform that implicitly eases platform workers access to unemployment benefits by allowing all types of income and not just waged-work to account towards individuals accrued rights. Likewise, some social partners have started to negotiate collective agreements covering especially labour platforms to strengthen such individual's safety net when operating online (Ilsøe and Madsen 2018). However, further configurations of existing welfare and IR-arrangements seem to be needed to cover the protective gaps, where relaxed eligibility criteria in terms of lowering the threshold for past employment records and number of hours worked may be a way forward to cushion the risks of precariousness, especially among those working for low income on labour platforms.

On the other hand, our findings suggest that the Danish social assistance and unemployment benefit schemes along with the knock-on effects of the collectively agreed wages on the unregulated labour market may also limit downward pressures on price setting on the digital platforms. They implicitly provide an informal wage floor, which is difficult for the platforms to ignore if they want to attract individuals to sell their services via the platform. Therefore, the established Danish welfare and IR-systems seemingly and to some extent prevent employers from utilising labour platforms to circumvent the existing labour market system to curb labour costs, as much of digital platform literature argues and seen with the recent rise of other forms of atypical employment in several countries (Rubery 2015; Berg 2016; Kalleberg and Vallas 2018). Our findings support this notion, as most individuals active on labour platforms complement their scarce income generated via the platform with unemployment benefits, social assistance, or other welfare-regulated social benefits. Optimists would argue that platforms foster labour market inclusion and that we have only seen the beginning of this potential – platform services will grow and contribute to growth and employment – for marginalised as well as other groups. Pessimists, however, would look at the risks of precariousness, especially in countries where the wider institutional framework fails to deliver a buffer that counteracts the weak regulatory framework characterising the digital platforms (Wood et al. 2019). Further studies, including longitudinal data on platform providers, their employment status and income, can tell us, whether platform work over time contributes to labour market integration or segmentation. Such studies might also include other variables as indicators of precariousness than the classic demographic variables used in previous studies (Kalleberg 2011; Thelen 2019). This could be variables on health and safety issues, stress and perceived employment insecurity (Gash et al. 2007). Our study offers important conceptual and methodological insights and experiences that can be of relevance for such future research. Firstly, the conceptual distinction between labour and capital platforms is crucial as these platforms attract very different crowds. Secondly, it is important to include both forms in future research to investigate their various effects since not only labour platforms, but also capital platforms may influence the structure and composition of the future labour market and its regulation.

Notes

1 There are always some uncertainties associated with using sample data. Statistics Denmark deals with selection bias in two ways. Firstly, all analyses are based on a weighted sample, which means that the results can be said to be a representative expression of the entire Danish population. Secondly, numbers representing fewer than 7,000 individuals are reported as uncertain in the analysis – and numbers representing fewer than 4,000 individuals are not displayed (Statistics Denmark 2012).
2 We included these variables since most studies on precarious employment indicate that they play a key role in determining the risks of precariousness (Kalleberg 2011; Thelen 2019). Due to a small NN, the variable 'total income of employed citizens' could only be included in the descriptive statistics.
3 www.skat.dk/skat.aspx?oid=2236769.
4 In Spring 2018, the Danish union 3F (United Federation of Danish Workers) and the cleaning platform Hilfr signed a collective agreement which, among other things, sets a minimum wage and different labour standards.
5 Source: happyhelper.dk.
6 Source: hilfr.dk.
7 This might seem counter intuitive, but platform work is rarely registered in the traditional administrative Danish registers, which means that citizens can be registered as out of work and participate on labour platforms at the same time.

References

Aleksynska, M., Bastrakova, A. and Karchenko, N. (2018) *Work on Digital Labour Platforms in Ukraine*. Geneva: ILO.

Berg, J. (2016) *Income Security in the on-Demand Economy*. Geneva: ILO.

Campbell, I. and Price, R. (2016) 'Precarious work and precarious workers'. *The Economic and Labour Relations Review*, 37(3): 314–332.

Collier, R.B., Dubal, V.B. and Carter, C. (2017) 'Labor Platforms and Gig Work'. *IRLE Working Paper No. 106–117*.

De Groen, W.B. and Maselli, I. (2016) *The Impact of the Collaborative Economy on the Labour Market*. CEPS, Brussels: European Commission.

De Stefano, V. (2016) 'Introduction: crowdsourcing, the gig-economy and the law'. *Comparative Labor Law & Policy Journal*, 37(3): 461–470.

Degryse, C. (2017) 'Digitalisation of the Economy and its Impact on Labour Markets'. *Working paper 201602*, Brussels: ETUI.

DI, 3f and Service forbundet. (2017) *Serviceoverenskomsten*. Copenhagen: DI.

Doellgast, V., Lillie, N. and Pulignano, V. (eds) (2018) *Reconstructing Solidarity*. Oxford: Oxford University Press.

Due, J. and Madsen, J.S. (2008) 'The Danish model of industrial relations'. *Journal of Industrial Relations*, 50(3): 513–529.

Eichhorst, W. and Marx, P. (eds) (2015) *Non-standard Employment in Post-industrial Labour Markets*. Cheltenham: Edward Elgar.

Ejrnæs, A. (2006) 'Fleksibilitet og etnisk segregering'. *Dansk Sociologi*, 17(1): 21–40.

Emmenegger, P., Hausermann, S., Palier, B. and Seeleib-Kaiser, M. (2012) *The Age of Dualization*. Oxford: Oxford University Press.

Esping-Andersen, G. (1999) *Social Foundations of Postindustrial Economies*. Oxford: Oxford University Press.

European Commission. (2016) *A European Agenda for the Collaborative Economy*. Brussels: European Commission.

Farrell, D. and Greig, F. (2016) *Paychecks, Paydays, and the Online Platform Economy*. Washington, DC: The JPMorgan Chase Institute.

Fuchs, C. and Sevignani, S. (2013) 'What is digital labour'. *Triple C*, 11(2): 237–293.

Gash, V., Mertens, A. and Romeu-Gordo, L. (2007) 'Are fixed-term jobs bad for your health? A comparison of Spain and Germany'. *European Societies*, 9(3): 429–458.

Goods, C., Veen, A. and Barratt, T. (2019) 'Is your gig any good?' *Journal of Industrial Relations*, online first 10.1177/0022185618817069.

Grimshaw, D., Johnson, M., Rubery, J. and Arjan, K. (2016) *Reducing Precarious Work*. UK: University of Manchester.

Healy, J., Nicholson, D. and Pekarek, A. (2017) 'Should we take the gig economy seriously?' *Labour & Industry*, 27(3): 232–248.

Howcroft, D. and Bregvall-Kåreborn, B. (2019) 'A typology of crowdwork platforms'. *Work Employment and Society*, 33(1): 21–38.

Ilsøe, A., Larsen, T.P. and Felbo-Kolding, J. (2017) 'Living hours under pressure'. *Employee Relations*, 39(6): 888–902.

Ilsøe, A. and Madsen, L.W. (2017) *Digitalisering af Arbejdsmarkedet*. Copenhagen: University of Copenhagen.

Ilsøe, A. and Madsen, L.W. (2018) *Industrial Relations and Social Dialogue in the Age of Collaborative Economy*. Copenhagen: Copenhagen University.

Kalleberg, A. (2011) *Good Jobs, Bad Jobs*. New York: Russell Sage Foundation.

Kalleberg, A. and Vallas, S.P. (2018) 'Probing precarious work'. *Research in the Sociology of Work*, 31(1): 1–30.

Katz, L.F. and Krueger, A.B. (2016) *The Rise and Nature of Alternative Work Arrangements in the United States, 1995–2015*. Boston: Harvard University.

Keune, M. and Pedaci, M. (2019) 'Trade union strategies against precarious work'. *European Journal of Industrial Relations*, online https://doi.org/10.1177/0959680119827182.

Larsen, T.P., Navrbjerg, S.E. and andJohansen, M.M. (2010) *Tillidsrepræsentanten og arbejds-pladsen*. rapport 1. Copenhagen: LO.

Larsen, T.P. (2011) *Insidere og outsidere*. Copenhagen: DJØF Publishing.

Larsen, T.P. and Mailand, M. (2018) 'Lifting wages and conditions of atypical employees in Denmark'. *Industrial Relations Journal*, 49(2): 88–108.

LO. (2016) *Platformsøkonomi – lovgivningsmæssige udfordringer og fagbevægelsens løsningsforslag*. Copenhagen: LO.

Mailand, M. and Larsen, T.P. (2018) 'Hybrid Work- Social Protection of Atypical Employment in Denmark'. *WSI report*, Berlin: Hans-Böckler-Stiftung.

Palier, B. (2018) 'The politics of social risks and social protection in digitalised economies'. in Neufeind, M., O'Reilly, J., and Ranft, F. (eds). *Work in the Digital Age*. London: Rowman & Littlefield International, pp. 247–258.

Palier, B. and Thelen, K. (2010) 'Institutionalizing dualism'. *Politics & Society*, 38(1): 119–148.

Rubery, J. (2015) 'Change at work'. *Employee Relations*, 37(6): 633–644.

Rubery, J., Grimshaw, D., Keizer, A. and Johnson, M. (2018) 'Challenges and contradic-tions in the normalizing of precarious work'. *Work Employment and Society*, 32(3): 509–527.

Scheuer, S. (2017) 'Atypisk Beskæftigelse i Danmark'. *Lo-Dokumentation Nr. 1/2017*.

Schmidt, F. (2017) *Digital Labour Markets in the Platform Economy*. Bonn: Friedrich-Ebert Stiftung.

Schor, J.B. (2016) 'Debating the sharing economy'. *Journal of Self-Governance and Management Economics*, 4(3): 7–22.

Schor, J.B. and Attwood-Charles, W. (2017) 'The "sharing" economy'. *Sociology Compass*, 11(8): 1–16.

Söderqvist, F. (2017) 'A Nordic approach to regulating intermediary online labour platforms'. *Transfer*, 23(3): 349–352.

Statistics Denmark. (2012) *Uddybende notat vedr. brugen af AKU-mikrodata*. Copenhagen: Statistics Denmark.

Thelen, K. (2019) 'The American precariat'. *Perspectives on Politics*, 17(1): 5–27.

Thelen, K. and Weidemann, A. (2018) 'The Anxiety of Precarity, manuscript presented at the workshop "Anxieties of Democracy Project"'. Yale University December 2018.

Wood, A.J., Graham, M., Lehdonvirta, V. and Hjorth, I. (2019) 'Good gig, bad gig: autonomy and algorithmic control in the global gig economy'. *Work, Employment and Society*, 33(1): 56–75.

2 Do you trust sharing your finances and financing?

Christina Öberg

Introduction

During the past ten years, the sharing economy, that is, digitally-intermediated exchanges among peers (Belk, 2014), has expanded into yet new sectors, often marked by standardised services with low personal involvement and risk (Öberg, 2018c). One of those sectors to which the sharing economy has expanded is the financial sector. Platforms such as *Trustbuddy*, *Toborrow*, and *Lendify* mark this development, though with quite different ways of operating (cf. Mair & Reischauer, 2017 on the plurality of the sharing economy), and also with various levels of success.

Trust is suggested as being at the heart of the sharing economy (Ert, Fleischer, & Magen, 2016) and could be related to the different platforms' abilities to attract providing and using parties: ingredients essential for the success and continuity of the platforms. Based on how different financial sharing economy platforms have chosen different ways to operate (e.g., in terms of who chooses whom among providers and users, the platform taking a pronounced or more limited role in these regards, and how interest rates and investment objects are chosen and distributed), this chapter sets to *explain success and failure of financial sharing economy operations*. The unit of analysis is the triadic interaction among the provider, user, and platform, and the various ways of operating are described as business model designs (e.g., Andreassen et al., 2018; Osterwalder, Pigneur, & Tucci, 2005).

Empirically, this chapter analyses business-model designs and trust-establishing activities of a number of financial sharing-economy platforms. Contributions are made to the extant literature on the sharing economy through specifically focusing on financial platforms and through interlinking business model design with performance. These findings are important for the future development and expansion of the sharing economy, its impact on traditional financial services, and their possible adaptation to platform-related operations, and are specifically important for parties introducing new platforms using the sharing economy's operational designs. These implications are discussed in the chapter.

Theoretical background

Business model design in the sharing economy

A business model defines how a company operates its business, including its resource provision, ways to address customers, internal processes, and ways to earn income (e.g., Baden-Fuller & Morgan, 2010; Magretta, 2002; Osterwalder et al., 2005; Zott & Amit, 2010). The literature has pointed to how a business model may include several parties, rather than just a single firm (Chesbrough, 2006; Vanhaverbeke & Chesbrough, 2014; Zott & Amit, 2013), and the sharing-economy business model would be characterised by the distribution of processes among the provider, user and platform (Andreassen et al., 2018). The characterising traits include how the platform intermediates the exchanges between the provider and user, and how the sharing-economy business models may include overlapping parties in terms of peers as providers and users (Belk, 2014). Beyond this, activities may be distributed in different ways among the provider, user and platform, and the activities may also vary (Öberg, 2018b), which means that the business model design varies and creates a plurality in the sharing economy (Mair & Reischauer, 2017).

To capture business model design, researchers have focused on activities pursued (Zott & Amit, 2010), value creation and value capturing processes (Osterwalder & Pigneur, 2010), or aimed at the revenue side of business models only (Burger & Fuchs, 2005; Magretta, 2002). One of the most well-spread ways of describing business model design is the business model canvas (Osterwalder & Pigneur, 2010) reflecting value creating provision, the offering, and value capturing customer/market interaction, along with cost structures and revenue streams. Another, which puts focus on what parties do and how they do so, is the activity-based business model introduced by Zott and Amit (2010). This way of portraying business models puts focus on content, structure, and governance, and thereby helps to analyse how activities are distributed among different parties, as would be the case in the sharing economy. Content refers to what activities are pursued (such as whether evaluation is part of the business model). Structure defines how individual activities are interlinked (such as booking and execution processes as pre-processes and the main processes of exchange). Governance, lastly, points to who performs these activities and thereby helps to determine their distribution among providers, users and the platform in the sharing economy.

Trust in the sharing economy

A key component of any business exchange is trust. Trust refers to a party's (the trustor's) belief that another party (the trustee) will meet expectations in its future way of acting (Rousseau, Sitkin, Burt, & Camerer, 1998). It has been outlined based on its antecedents and components (Huemer, 1998), and connected to continued exchanges among parties (Fulmer & Gelfand, 2012; Rousseau et al., 1998; Schoorman, Mayer, & Davis, 2007). Mayer, Davis, and Schoorman (1995), as one of the most referred to definitions of trust, explain it based on abilities (skills of the trustee), benevolence (perception of the trustee), and integrity (acceptable behaviour of the trustee). McAllister (1995) describes trust as cognition-based (rational) and affective (emotional), respectively (cf. Smith & Lohrke, 2008). And, Sako (1992) refers to contractual trust (agreements made), competence-based trust (expected skills of the trustee), and goodwill trust (expected behaviour of the trustee). Taken together, this indicates how trust includes both judgments of skills and more affective evaluations of the other party (cf. Hasche, Linton, & Öberg, 2017). It also generally assumes how trust is established in two-party systems including the trustor and the trustee, both being operating parties (companies or individuals).

In the sharing economy, trust has been discussed as an antecedent to use services provided (Boateng, Kosiba, & Okoe, 2019; Forno & Garibaldi, 2015; Pappas, 2017; Tussyadiah & Pesonen, 2018), and specifically, to repeatedly do so (Mohlmann, 2015; Wang & Jeong, 2018). Compared to the two-party system of a trustor and trustee, the sharing economy creates a transactional, arm's-length way of operating, where the trustor rarely establishes a long-term or repeated exchange with the trustee, but rather does so with the platform as the intermediary. Again, and while being involved in transactional exchanges, measures have been taken to create components that would also affect the likelihood to create trust between the user and provider. More precisely, in the literature on trust in the sharing economy, trust is described to be linked to the personalisation of providers, such as profile photos (Ert et al., 2016) and descriptions (Cho, Park, & Kim, 2019; Zhang, Yan, & Zhang, 2018; Zloteanu, Harvey, Tuckett, & Livan, 2018), the peer-to-peer feedback of evaluations (Cheng, Fu, Sun, Bilgihan, & Okumus, 2019; Dredge & Gyimothy, 2015; Xie & Mao, 2017) and reciprocity between provider and user (Celata, Hendrickson, & Sanna, 2017; Lan, Ma, Zhu, Mangalagiu, & Thornton, 2017). The reciprocity refers to how providers become trusted through also acting as users, but also based on how those operating as part of the sharing economy create a culture or value system of honesty among them, which could be linked to the affective evaluation of trust (Hasche et al., 2017; McAllister, 1995; Smith & Lohrke, 2008). Hartl, Hofmann, and Kirchler (2016) link trust to personal traits, pointing to how trusting users prefer less governance of the sharing economy than do those not being as trust-reliant, thereby touching upon whether trust would be created through controls or rather soft value systems, and also pointing to how the sharing economy may only attract those parties more probable to trust others.

Most examples in research on trust in the sharing economy concern trust related to the accommodation platform *Airbnb*, and trust antecedents are usually empirically derived pointing at specifics related to the presentation of providers (hosts). Cheng et al. (2019), as one of very few exceptions, link trust in the sharing economy to the dimensions presented by Mayer et al. (1995):

abilities, benevolence, and integrity, where location and room design are linked to abilities, host attributes to benevolence, and room description to integrity, thereby also indicating the skill or attributive (what is offered) dimension of trust and the more affective one (related to likeability of the offering).

Trust and business model design in the sharing economy

Trust is thus different in the sharing economy compared to other exchanges, and is so in the following regards: (1) trust needs to be created between strangers meeting in quite ad-hoc transactional exchanges intermediated by an on-line third party (cf. Etzioni, 2019 on cyber trust), (2) trust is democratised in how it is distributed among peers (Hou, 2018) and partly created through third-party evaluations, and (3) the platform may be the trustee or the intermediary for trust evaluations and trust-establishing presentations. Based on how a business model can be understood as an activity system with content, structures and governance as components to analyse its design (Zott & Amit, 2010), it would also be possible to interlink the business model design with the discussion on trust, and then specifically what activities are pursued and how they are distributed among parties as antecedents to trust in its skill and affective dimensions.

Research design

This chapter analyses financial sharing-economy business models and whether and how these create trust based on their designs, with the purpose to explain the success and failure of financial sharing economy operations. To empirically do so, the author started by searching for financial sharing economy platforms. This rested on the following search methods: (1) a social media data analysis compiling all posts including the term "the sharing economy" in Sweden and platforms referred to in these posts (cf. Geissinger, Laurell, Öberg, & Sandström, 2019), (2) a *Web of Science* journal article database search including "finance"/"financial" and "sharing economy" followed by visits to articles found and a list created based on those empirical examples listed in these articles, and (3) financial sharing economy platforms known by the author. These last items were either collected based on previous studies by the author or known examples from the Swedish press. While these three search methods created an overweight of Swedish financial sharing economy platforms, or platforms operating in Sweden, they also allowed for the compilation of financial information on these platforms, based on such data being public in Sweden. The focus on Sweden was also considered positive based on how the country frequently is described as a forerunner in its entrepreneurial ambitions, with plenty of sharing economy platforms having been created during the past years.

Once the list of financial sharing economy platforms was constructed, the websites and apps of these platforms were tracked so as to capture the business-model design of each. Using Zott and Amit's (2010) description of content, structure and governance, the business models were analysed in the dimensions of activities pursued, how they were linked, and how they were distributed among users, providers, and the platform. If the websites or apps did not provide enough information, newspaper searches were performed for details. Annual reports were thereafter addressed to capture revenues and EBITA (operating profit) results of the platforms and their developments over the past five years (if the platform had existed for that long) to capture the success related to each business-model design). For platforms no longer in practice, database searches included comments on bankruptcies or financial problems of the platforms.

Once data had been compiled for each platform, it was compared to find patterns between business-model design and trust-establishing activities. Platforms adopting similar designs were thereby aggregated into clustered groups. The process of creating clusters involved several rounds of comparisons among the individual business models so as to create meaningful clusters of similarities. To exemplify the creation of clusters, similarities among the core idea of the business model (financing specific projects or borrowing/lending for financial planning purposes, for instance), how activities were distributed among users, providers and platforms, and what evaluation tools were in place and operated by whom created distinguishing characteristics. The clusters were then used to see whether and how they also represented similarities in trust-establishing activities, and were, if possible, linked to financial results of the platforms (revenues and operating profit/loss). If no such pattern presented itself between individual platforms, they were carried forward as separate groups to be addressed with how they differed in their design or trust-imposing constructs. However, and as indicated by the Findings section, three quite distinct archetypes could be grasped using these methods of clustering and also revealing similarities between business model designs and trust-imposing constructs.

Based on the clustering of the business models, it was possible to draw some conclusions on how financial sharing-economy business models should best be designed, but also on mistakes made discrediting any trust establishments. This part of the analysis included iterated dimensions of the division of activities between parties (essentially between peers and platforms), and what activities needed to be present. Furthermore, and derived from the analysis of press material on the platforms, activities pursued so as to show how the platform handled any upcoming issues affecting trust were seen as mediating activities external to the actual business-model design. As a last step of analysis, findings were compared with previous research on sharing-economy business models and trust in relation to the sharing economy. This was done to ensure the covering of a research gap and to formulate the contribution to previous research.

Findings and analysis

Table 2.1 presents the individual business models named after the intermediary platforms in each identified example. The platforms span from crowdfunding operations intermediated through platforms over automated investment services (robo-advice) to platforms carrying many similarities with conventional banks. Again, these various designs (and also partially contents of operations) are also linked to quite different distributions of activities among the provider, user and platform, and also partially contain some differences in activities.

Relating the business models designs to Zott and Amit's (2010) description on business models as activity systems, three archetypes are found:

• Business models with the financing of a specific idea in focus (*active investment business model*). Here, activities are extensive, focusing much on pre-exchange presentations and with the user (borrower) as the active party, while the platform essentially becomes a window to display ideas and attract providers' (lenders') interests. *Kickstarter, Crofun*, and *FundedByMe* are part of this category. Trust is essentially created based on the user's presentations of ideas, credit history and her/himself, and thereby largely becomes unilateral: it is the provider that needs to start trusting the user, and evaluations of trust would be affective to high degrees (cf. Hasche et al., 2017; McAllister, 1995; Smith & Lohrke, 2008) related to integrity (cf. Mayer et al., 1995) and goodwill (Sako, 1992), based on expectations of the future idea and the user's ability to realise it.
• Business models copying banks (*banking-clone business model*), but trying to be the alternative to conventional banks. Here, activities are limited to investment savings and loans, with the platform coordinating users and providers knowing very little about each other. The platform thereby becomes the essential party to create trust in operations. There seems to be the trend that these platforms either source from or connect to conventional banks or established financial actors, which creates trust for the platform. They also increasingly use the same evaluation tools for creditability of borrowers as do the conventional banks. *LendingClub, Zelle*, and *Prosper* exemplify this category.
• Hybrid business models of the above (*the hybrid business model*), focusing on the financial transactions (rather than investments in specific ideas), while linking to such ideas and the provider's evaluation of the user. Here, the user and provider become the most active parties and activities also link to describing intentions, etc., to create trust in the user and its motives. Some platforms combine this business model design with the bank-clone option and allow the provider to either make portfolio investments or select a certain borrower. Interest rates would thereby also vary depending on options, where the active choice of a borrower mostly suggests including the provider and user agreeing on the interest rate, while it is pre-set by the platform in the bank-clone business models. Table 2.2 summarises the three defined business model designs and their activities, as well as how trust is created related to each of them.

Table 2.1 Financial sharing-economy business models

	Lendify	Trustbuddy	Toborrow	Savy	LendingClub	Lufax	FundedByMe
Description of operations	Borrowing/saving where the party saving may choose a specific borrower or have her/his saving distributed among 40 parties	Micro-borrowing where loans are compiled of providers' placement of funding	Reverse auction between provider and user, where the provider presents itself and intention with the loan and saver bids an amount and interest rate. Borrower then selects those requesting the lowest interest rate	Private loan facilitation. Primary and secondary market loans	Investment and loan options where the platform evaluates loan application and the saver decides more or less activity in selecting or allowing the platform to spread risk	Provides funding to loans through the presentation of borrowers' requests	Funding specifically directed at start-ups and early growth companies (crowdfunding)
Country	Sweden	Sweden	Sweden	Baltic states	USA	China	Sweden
User (borrower)	Places application	Borrowing amount. Active in selecting	Places description of itself, purpose of loan and amount	Decides amount and interest rates	Places request for amount to borrow	Places wished amount to borrow on platform	Presents product/idea and need for financing along with the company. Issues shares
Provider (saver)	Places money either through selecting borrower or having the platform spread it among borrowers	Puts funding into the system. No selection of borrower	Bids in auction: interest rate and amount. Selects borrower	Invests directly to borrower	Provides funding. The platform divides these into 25USD mini-loans that the provider places by different borrowers	Bids for borrower's loan	Decides on investments based on their presentations. Become partial owners
Platform	Evaluates borrower. Distributes funds from saver. Sets interest rates	Coordination of loans	Intermediates information and loans	Sets credit rate of borrower. Facilitates second market	Approval of loans, sets interest rates, servicing and support operations	Displays loan requests, intermediates transactions	Displays information on investment opportunities

(Continued)

Table 2.1 (Cont.)

	Lendify	Trustbuddy	Toborrow	Savy	LendingClub	Lufax	FundedByMe
Trust	Spread of risk among borrowers. Display of judgement of service (the platform) on website. Owners of platform	Fraud by the platform undermined any trust established	Essentially through presentations of borrower. When one did not pay back, the platform covered this. Partly owned by financial actor	Transparency of description of borrower (personal data)	Distribution of risk through fractions of savings going into different loans	All transactions being made through the platform	Thorough description of investment options
Financial performance	Revenues: 25MSEK; Profit: -52MSEK (2017)	Bankrupt	Revenues: 0,4MSEK; Profit: – 8 MSEK	-	Revenues: 182MUSD; Profit: 98 MUSD	-	Revenues: 14MSEK; Profit: -15MSEK

(Continued)

Table 2.1 (Contd.)

	Zelle/ClearXchange	Betterment	Crofun	Zopa	Prosper	SmartyPig	Kickstarter
Description of operations	As part of regular banking (Capital One), offering peer-to-peer lending	Investor advisor targeting investors (providers) with various levels of skills/confidence to make investment decisions Robo-advice	Crowdfunding and investment platform focusing on business projects. Including social lending and donations	Lending platform	Connects borrowers and lenders	Social savings bank aimed at engaging friends to contribute	Funding platform for business projects in early phases
Country	USA	USA	Belgium	UK	USA	USA	USA
User (borrower)	Making payments into accounts of providers	–	Presents idea to be funded	Borrows money through the platform	Provide information on themselves and credit history	Same as saver, potentially trying to make parties donate	Places description of business idea and need for funding. Markets the project
Provider (saver)	Receives funds	Places funding based on advice from the platform and related to the purpose of saving	Provides money as investment for shares, loans, donations, etc.	Places funding against monthly interest returns	Decides whom to lend money	Sets up account and targets for savings. Presents and distributes these to friends	Invests in projects based on descriptions, often with a user interest to be able to use the product further on
Platform	A means for direct payment between parties (these mostly knowing one another beforehand)	Provides advice on investments and tax issues. Suggests portfolios	Presents ideas and creates links between providing and using party	Coordinates borrowing and lending. Transfers interests	Calculates interest rate based on risk scoring of borrower. Provides score of borrowers and creates portfolios as an option to the provider selecting the borrower	Makes investments to yield return	Presents borrowers' ideas. Creates rules for transactions (all or nothing)

(Continued)

Table 2.1 (Cont.)

	Zelle/ ClearXchange	Bettement	Crofun	Zopa	Prosper	SmartyPig	Kickstarter
Trust	Provider and user knowing one another beforehand. Transfer of money essentially. Owned by regular bank	Trust established through previous performance of the platform	Trust essentially based on borrower's description of idea and based on social engagement in ideas	Bank license of platform	Information provided by the borrower and credit score provided by the platform	Essentially accredited by the saver	Essentially based on the project as such
Financial performance	-	-	-	-	-	-	-

Table 2.2 Summary of archetypes

	Active investments	Bank clone	The hybrid
Content	Presentations and pre-investment evaluations in focus	Decision on interest rates and credibility evaluations of borrowers	Focus on financial returns and ability to borrow
Structure	Pre-processes leading to money transaction and provision of interests, idea, or other incentives as post-processes	Focus on main process: the lending/borrowing	Pre-process may be important as the provider can choose level of activity
Governance	Relies heavily on the user and provider	Relies on the platform to decide interest rates, credit scores, etc.	Relies on the user and provider, with the platform performing more or fewer activities depending on choices of the provider
Trust	Largely the provider's trust in the user or the user's idea. Affective to a large extent	Largely reliant on the bank and often connected to it being (or over time becoming) financially institutionalised	Reliant on the platform and the user, respectively

Linking the various archetypes to the financial performances of the platforms, it should first be said that the financial performances were only possible to trace for a few platforms, while the survival of the platform operations, their expansions and their developments over time give some further indications. *Zopa*, for instance, has been around for almost 15 years, while *Trustbuddy* thus ended up in bankruptcy five years ago. A commonality for those platforms where financial data could be found is how they have expanded year-by-year, but still rely on external funding (venture capital) in their efforts to become successful. As a matter of fact, *Lendify*, *Toborrow*, and *FundedByMe* all showed losses for the past years. Developments suggest an increased institutionalisation with financial institutions becoming partial owners in many of these, and other cases. Again, this also means that the platforms transform to increasingly resemble banks, while some platforms have indeed added the active choices of providers to their business models.

From an expansion point of view, the bank clones have been more successful in growing their operations, and such expansion has also, in other examples (beyond the financial sharing-economy business models), been linked to how the platform conducts most of the activities and increasingly addresses trust issues (see, for instance, the development of *Airbnb* and *Uber*, Öberg, 2018a).

Conclusions

This chapter explains the success and failure of financial sharing economy operations through linking business-model design to trust. It points at three archetypes: the active-investment, the bank-clone, and the hybrid sharing-economy business models, and how trust becomes mainly linked to the borrower or the platform. Again, this creates a variation between affective and skill-related trust, where the more active investments link more to affective evaluations of goodwill trust or integrity (cf. Mayer et al., 1995; Sako, 1992), and bank-clone business models link to rational, contractual, skill-based trust (cf. Mayer et al., 1995; McAllister, 1995; Sako, 1992) related to past behaviours. Again, there is also the suggested link between the type of trust, whether the trust is primarily linked to the user (the borrower) or the platform, with affective trust being connected with the borrower, and rational, contractual, skill-based trust related to the platform. Operations suggest that the trustee is also the party that performs most of the activities, with active investments relying heavily on activities of the borrower, and the bank-clone business model depending largely on the platform. This last circumstance again suggests being linked to the scalability of operations.

Implications of findings

Those business models constructing the empirical part of this chapter may, to some extent, be questioned as to whether they represent sharing-economy business models. The crowdfunding platforms indeed share the characteristics of an intermediary platform, while the stranger-to-stranger, arm's-length transactional orientation of exchanges is not as evident. Rather, as a starting point or to be accomplished in the trust-establishing pre-investment processes, attempts are made to decrease distance, socialise the exchange and also pave the way for an investment with some time horizon. This is again denoted in how trust needs to be established for the borrower and how these types of exchanges may rely on motives of creating good (such as creating ideas that are good for the society).

The bank-clone business models often rely on an institutional player as the platform (or as an owner of it), and could thereby equally be questioned as to which extent it is a sharing economy operation. Furthermore, over the years, the inclusion of companies as investors and borrowers has risen. Still, most of these business models include an intermediary platform and exchanges remain transactional, while they often do not connect the user and the provider at all.

With this said, there is a plurality of business models (Mair & Reischauer, 2017) also in the financial sharing economy, and while many of these business models develop over time, they seem to continuously represent the spread from active investments relying on affective trust evaluations of borrowers, to the bank-clone operations with the platform carrying most of the activities and also the trust-establishing traits.

For conventional financial institutions, the development of a financial sharing economy could and has partly created grounds to inspire creations of new business models, while these do not suggest to expand beyond the bank-clone business model design. Active investments, crowdfunding and social causes for lending and borrowing may be trends to increasingly pick up by banks, or to inspire for business developments. The risks (and trust-establishing traits) largely being carried by borrowers would here construct opportunities that would allow the financial institutions to remain silent parties in this potential expansion of business. With that said, the financial sharing-economy business models compete with traditional financial institutions, not the least for parties wanting to oppose established structures, but also receive higher interest rates, and obtain loans or funding not achieved from banks. With an increase of businesses being run as idea-based, service firms, this portion of loans and funding could expect to increase, and thereby create a growing competing force vis-à-vis established actors in the financial sector.

In the long-term perspective, the financial sharing-economy business models may well change values of both lenders' and borrowers' view on trust and how the financial system should best be operated, meaning that banks may be obsolete to some extent. For society, the more distributed the financial sector, the less the control, but also the broader the allowance for new establishments to emerge, both as financial actors and as businesses and other organisations borrowing and lending through these parties. Tax issues have been widely discussed in relation to the sharing economy, and while the platforms operate as professional business models, other types of regulatory regimes may over time be questioned or even set aside as the financial sharing-economy business model spread and develop. Thus, new business models may cause societal changes and also changes to values, as well as be driven by such.

References

Andreassen, T.W., Lervik-Olsen, L., Snyder, H., Van Riel, A.C.R., Sweeney, J.C., & Van Vaerenbergh, Y. (2018). Business model innovation and value-creation: the triadic way. *Journal of Service Management, 29*(5), 883–906.

Baden-Fuller, C., & Morgan, M.S. (2010). Business models as models. *Long Range Planning, 43*(2–3), 156–171.

Belk, R. (2014). You are what you can access: sharing and collaborative consumption online. *Journal of Business Research, 67*(8), 1595–1600.

Boateng, H., Kosiba, J.P.B., & Okoe, A.F. (2019). Determinants of consumers' participation in the sharing economy: A social exchange perspective within an emerging economy context. *International Journal of Contemporary Hospitality Management, 31*(2), 718–733.

Burger, B., & Fuchs, M. (2005). Dynamic pricing: a future airline business model. *Journal of Revenue & Pricing Management, 4*(1), 39–53.

Celata, F., Hendrickson, C.Y., & Sanna, V.S. (2017). The sharing economy as community marketplace? Trust, reciprocity and belonging in peer-to-peer accommodation platforms. *Cambridge Journal of Regions Economy and Society, 10*(2), 349–363.

Cheng, X.S., Fu, S.X., Sun, J.S., Bilgihan, A., & Okumus, F. (2019). An investigation on online reviews in sharing economy driven hospitality platforms: A viewpoint of trust. *Tourism Management, 71*, 366–377.

Chesbrough, H.W. (2006). *Open business models: How to thrive in the new innovation landscape.* Boston, MA: Harvard Business School Press.

Cho, S., Park, C., & Kim, J. (2019). Leveraging consumption intention with identity information on sharing economy platforms. *Journal of Computer Information Systems, 59*(2), 178–187.

Dredge, D., & Gyimothy, S. (2015). The collaborative economy and tourism: Critical perspectives, questionable claims and silenced voices. *Tourism Recreation Research, 40*(3), 286–302.

Ert, E., Fleischer, A., & Magen, N. (2016). Trust and reputation in the sharing economy: The role of personal photos in Airbnb. *Tourism Management, 55*, 62–73.

Etzioni, A. (2019). Cyber trust. *Journal of Business Ethics, 156*(1), 1–13.

Forno, F., & Garibaldi, R. (2015). Sharing economy in travel and tourism: The case of home-swapping in Italy. *Journal of Quality Assurance in Hospitality & Tourism, 16*(2), 202–220.

Fulmer, C.A., & Gelfand, M.J. (2012). At what level (and in whom) we trust: Trust across multiple organizational levels. *Journal of Management, 38*(4), 1167–1230.

Geissinger, A., Laurell, C., Öberg, C., & Sandström, C. (2019). How sustainable is the sharing economy?: On the sustainability connotations of sharing economy platforms. *Journal of Cleaner Production, 206*, 419–429.

Hartl, B., Hofmann, E., & Kirchler, E. (2016). Do we need rules for "what's mine is yours"?: Governance in collaborative consumption communities. *Journal of Business Research, 69*(8), 2756–2763.

Hasche, N., Linton, G., & Öberg, C. (2017). Trust in open innovation: The case of a med-tech start-up. *European Journal of International Management, 20*(1), 31–49.

Hou, L.Y. (2018). Destructive sharing economy: A passage from status to contract. *Computer Law & Security Review, 34*(4), 965–976.

Huemer, L. (1998). *Trust in business relations: Economic logic or social interaction.* Umeå: Boréa Bokförlag.

Lan, J., Ma, Y., Zhu, D.J., Mangalagiu, D., & Thornton, T.F. (2017). Enabling value co-creation in the sharing economy: The case of mobike. *Sustainability, 9*, 9.

Magretta, J. (2002). Why business models matter. *Harvard Business Review, 80*(5), 86–92.

Mair, J., & Reischauer, G. (2017). Capturing the dynamics of the sharing economy: Institutional research on the plural forms and practices of sharing economy organizations. *Technological Forecasting and Social Change, 125*, 11–20.

Mayer, R.C., Davis, J.H., & Schoorman, D.F. (1995). An integrative model of organizational trust. *Academy of Management Review, 20*(3), 709–734.

McAllister, D.J. (1995). Affect – and cognition-based trust formations for interpersoanl cooperation in organizations. *Academy of Management Journal, 38*(1), 24–59.

Mohlmann, M. (2015). Collaborative consumption: determinants of satisfaction and the likelihood of using a sharing economy option again. *Journal of Consumer Behaviour, 14*(3), 193–207.

Öberg, C. (2018a). *Has the sharing economy become institutionalised?* Paper presented at the Paper Development Workshop for JMS' Special Issue: Challenges and Opportunities in the Sharing Economy, Beijing.

Öberg, C. (2018b). *Roles in the sharing economy.* Paper presented at the ISPIM, Stockholm.

Öberg, C. (2018c). Social and economic ties in the freelance and sharing economies. *Journal of Small Business and Entrepreneurship, 30*(1), 77–96.

Osterwalder, A., & Pigneur, Y. (2010). *Business model generation: a handbook for visionaries, game changers, and challengers.* Chichester: Wiley.

Osterwalder, A., Pigneur, Y., & Tucci, C. (2005). Clarifying business models: origins, present and future of the concept. *Communications of the Association for Information Systems, 15,* 751–775.

Pappas, N. (2017). The complexity of purchasing intentions in peer-to-peer accommodation. *International Journal of Contemporary Hospitality Management, 29*(9), 2302–2321.

Rousseau, D.M., Sitkin, S.B., Burt, R.S., & Camerer, C. (1998). Not so different after all: A cross-discipline view of trust. *Academy of Management Review, 23*(3), 393–404.

Sako, M. (1992). *Prices, quality and trust: inter-firm relations in Britain and Japan.* Cambridge, MA: Cambridge University Press.

Schoorman, D.F., Mayer, R.C., & Davis, J.H. (2007). An integrative model of organizational trust: past, present and future. *Academy of Management Review, 31*(2), 344–354.

Smith, D.A., & Lohrke, F.T. (2008). Entrepreneurial network development: trusting in the process. *Journal of Business Research, 61,* 315–322.

Tussyadiah, I.P., & Pesonen, J. (2018). Drivers and barriers of peer-to-peer accommodation stay: An exploratory study with American and Finnish travellers. *Current Issues in Tourism, 21*(6), 703–720.

Vanhaverbeke, W., & Chesbrough, H. (2014). A classification of open innovation and open business models. In H.W. Chesbrough, W. Vanhaverbeke & J. West (eds.), *New frontiers in open innovation* (pp. 50–68). Oxford: Oxford University Press.

Wang, C.H., & Jeong, M. (2018). What makes you choose Airbnb again?: An examination of users' perceptions toward the website and their stay. *International Journal of Hospitality Management, 74,* 162–170.

Xie, K.R., & Mao, Z.X. (2017). The impacts of quality and quantity attributes of Airbnb hosts on listing performance. *International Journal of Contemporary Hospitality Management, 29*(9), 2240–2260.

Zhang, L., Yan, Q., & Zhang, L.H. (2018). A computational framework for understanding antecedents of guests' perceived trust towards hosts on Airbnb. *Decision Support Systems, 115,* 105–116.

Zloteanu, M., Harvey, N., Tuckett, D., & Livan, G. (2018). Digital identity: the effect of trust and reputation information on user judgement in the sharing economy. *Plos One, 13,* 12.

Zott, C., & Amit, R. (2010). Business model design: an activity system perspective. *Long Range Planning, 43*(2–3), 216–226.

Zott, C., & Amit, R. (2013). The business model: a theoretically anchored robust construct for strategic analysis. *Strategic Organization, 11*(4), 403–411.

3 Trust, control, and risk in MaaS alliances

Elena Dybtsyna, Terje Andreas Mathisen, Bjørn-Anders Carlsson, and Kenneth Hardy

Introduction

More than half of the world's population lives in cities and this is expected to increase to two thirds by 2050 (Economist, 2016). The increase in people traveling within urban boundaries will increase problems of congestion and gridlock. Increasingly, people living in city centers are getting used to relying on public transport rather than using a private car. The idea of transport as a service is thus both natural and desirable, which makes it increasingly attractive as a product to be recognized as part of the concept of sharing economy.

The research on sharing economy is developing and several definitions of it have been proposed. The definition in the Oxford English Dictionary[1] follows: "an economic system in which assets or services are shared between private individuals, either free or for a fee, typically by means of the Internet." According to Parente et al. (2018, p. 52) the term "sharing economy" has been used frequently to describe different organizations that connect users/renters and owner/providers through consumer-to-consumer (C2C) (e.g., Uber, Airbnb) or business-to-consumer (B2C) platforms, allowing rentals in more flexible, social interactive terms (e.g., Zipcar, WeWork). Other terms such as "gig economy", "collaborative consumption", and "access-based economy" have also been used to characterize these for- and non-profit organizations. Strømmen-Bakhtiar and Vinogradov (2019, p. 88) state that these sharing economy solutions "provide an open, participative, plug-and-play infrastructure for producers and consumers to plug into and interact with each other; and they curate participants on the platform and govern the social and economic interactions that ensue". Goodall et al. (2017) makes a comparison between how people have adopted streaming in media and argues that transportation stands on a similar frontier.

Mobility as a Service (MaaS) could be one of the means to manage the increasing demand for transport in urban areas. There is, according to Mulley et al. (2018), still a limited focus on MaaS in the scholarly literature and there is no unified definition of the concept. What definitions have in common is the view of transport services as a shared or common transport solution as an alternative to transport by private car. Aarhaug (2017) states that the concept of MaaS has the objective of making mobility a service that is detached from the use of only a single mode of transportation. A mobility supplier will coordinate the different types of transport modes available and communicate this to the passenger using online technology solutions such as an app. Hence, MaaS as platform organization can engage users and providers in an efficient and transparent marketplace, where competition increases by offering consumers an attractive alternative or even replacing established players (see e.g., Parente et al., 2018). MaaS solutions, according to Aarhaug (2017) have been piloted in a number of larger European cities such as Helsinki and London.

In MaaS there are several ways to make the payment for the transport services – either as a subscription granting a limited number of vehicle kilometers or trips within a given time frame for a certain transport mode (Goodall et al., 2017) or as a single trip payment. According to Hensher (2017), the most important property is that MaaS offers passengers mobility based on individual transport needs.

Hensher (2017) states that MaaS is still under development and will incorporate technological advances such as autonomous driving. MaaS is thereby one element in the discussion of how public transport will be offered in the new digital reality with smart phones for easy access to both ordering and use of services. The concept of MaaS (see e.g., Goodall et al., 2017; Hensher, 2017) would thereby reduce the need for people to own a private car since transport from point to point can be provided by smart technology. Consequently, MaaS in the form of a platform organization and representing "collaborative consumption" makes use of market intelligence to foster a more collaborative and sustainable society (Heinrichs, 2013).

Parente et al. (2018) state that sharing economy firms function as an interface connecting different groups of users that interact through a virtual marketplace according to certain rules and guidelines. Combining the current research discourse on sharing economy with the context of the Norwegian transport sector operating on competitive tendering for the procurement of public transportation services may lead to a better understanding of how such platforms function in the case of a high degree of regulation by state authorities. This chapter will thereby contribute to the knowledge of how MaaS projects should be organized with the prospect of better projects leading to transport solutions supporting the overall objectives of sustainable development, which are represented, for example, in the UN Sustainable Development Goals[2] and thereby also reflected as the underlying basis for regulators' overall objectives.

In order to make new forms of transport solutions workable, there is a need for the various public transport modes to cooperate. Such cooperation could take the form of interorganizational cooperation, which, according to Das and Teng (1999), would have varying implications for the participants. However, the overall objective for firms entering into such alliances would be to improve the situation for the firm (Haugland, 2004). Another motivator for engaging in such an alliance, according to Johnson et al. (2017), is to gain access to resources and competence, making the firm able to achieve the objectives in a better way than would otherwise be possible when acting alone. In addition, as in the case of platform organizations, where one of the features is reduction in transaction costs related to matching a customer's need with potential providers (see e.g., Parente et al., 2018), strategic alliances can assist partner companies in implementing activities at reduced costs (Das & Teng, 1999). Johnson et al. (2017) classify strategic alliances according to whether firms have ownership in each other, such as joint ventures, minority equity alliances, and non-equity alliances. Engaging in an alliance with other firms is related to the challenges of trust, control, and risk, depending on the type of alliance. If the various actors do not put enough effort into reaching the objectives then engaging in an alliance may have a negative effect (Das & Teng, 1999). Consequently, trust, control, and risk are three critically important dimensions for a strategic alliance to succeed (Das & Teng, 2001). Moreover, failure to develop trust between users and partners in platform businesses has been identified as one of the common mistakes when considering a platform organization (see Yoffie et al., 2019). Thus, the interplay between trust, control, and risk in alliances is a relevant framework for analyzing MaaS as a platform, and also because this is a cooperation between public and private organizations, both for the actual service and for supporting activities, such as creating the smart phone application.

The aim of this chapter is to address the call for research with regard among other things, to trust building (Parente et al., 2018) and establishing trust (Strømmen-Bakhtiar & Vinogradov, 2019) by studying the interplay between trust, control, and risk in MaaS alliances. A theoretical approach is taken in the management control literature, our tool here for analyzing our empirical data from the transport industry in Norway. Norway is a relevant case because this is a mature market for technological infrastructure with the use of smart phones. There have been earlier studies on platform organization, such as Kornberger et al. (2017), focusing on evaluative infrastructures that enable platform-based organization. According to Strømmen-Bakhtiar and Vinogradov (2019) "sharing economy" or platform-based companies are disrupting the traditional industries. Such values as trust involved on eBay, skills at LinkedIn and reputation on Airbnb that need to be evaluated and none of these platforms have any warehouse where products are stored, nor concrete spaces (such as the factory floor). We differ from platform studies such as that by Kornberger et al. (2017) by focusing on the interplay between trust, control, and risk and from studies on strategic alliances such as that by Das and Teng (2001) and Schumacher (2006) by focusing on non-equity alliances.

The next section reviews the literature on strategic alliances with a focus on trust, control, and risk and concludes with a framework to be used in the discussion of our empirical evidence. Then we present our method for obtaining the data from the Norwegian transport industry before we in the next section connects the empirical evidence with the theoretical framework by means of analysis and discussion. Finally, in the last section we provide conclusions and implications.

Theoretical framework

This section discusses the relevant theory on interorganizational cooperation. Then we address the concept of strategic alliance with a focus on non-equity alliances and the motives for engaging in such a form of cooperation. This is relevant for MaaS solutions since contracts regulate how independent firms behave towards each other. Finally, we account for trust, control, and risk in strategic alliances and the interplay between these in formalized cooperation such as an alliance.

Interorganizational cooperation

Within the literature there exist several concepts explaining how companies engage in cooperation with other entities on both national and international levels. Some firms benefit greatly from such cooperation while others sustain substantial losses (Das & Teng, 1999). Haugland (2004) argues that the overall goal for the firm would be to strengthen its strategic position. That study demonstrates that firms engaged in interorganizational cooperation gain access to resources such as technology and competence or strengthen their position in the market.

`Strategic alliances are interfirm cooperative arrangements aimed at achieving the strategic objectives of the partners (Das & Teng, 1998). These alliances involve two or more partner firms with an element of interfirm cooperation. Strategic alliances assume many forms, such as joint ventures, minority equity alliances, and non-equity alliances. In addition, as in the case of a platform organization, where one of the features is reduction in transaction costs related to matching a customer's need with potential providers (see e.g., Parente et al., 2018), strategic alliances can assist partner companies to implement activities at reduced costs or if it is challenging to do this internally (Das & Teng, 1999). All forms of alliances have different regulations, which influence the interplay between trust, control, and risk (Das & Teng, 2001; Johnson et al., 2017).

The MaaS solutions in the Norwegian context, where publicly subsidized transport modes are represented by a strong public developer procuring services from independent firms by the use of competitive tendering is an example of non-equity alliances where contractual agreements do not involve any equity arrangement, so neither hierarchical nor ownership control is possible. In this type of alliance, the firms share their skills and resources to achieve a certain goal and gain a competitive advantage. Bierly and Coombs (2004) argue that non-equity alliances offer greater flexibility between partners, fewer commitments and are typically of shorter duration than other forms of cooperation. Examples are agreements regulated by contracts for the use of licenses and supplier contracts. The firms in the alliance operate as separate units according to the agreement concluded (Das & Teng, 1998). For this reason, the content of the contract is of vital importance. The control in such an alliance mainly concerns whether all partners adhere to the contract and do not operate in an opportunistic way to benefit themselves.

Risk

The main difference between entering a market using a single-firm strategy rather than through a strategic alliance is the uncertainty related to the cooperation among partners. There is always a level of relational risk in these alliances referring to the risk of a partner failing to cooperate in good faith. There is also a performance risk referring to the usual risk of satisfactory business performance (Das & Teng, 2001).

In strategic alliances, relational risk is defined as the probability and consequences of not having satisfactory cooperation (Das & Teng, 1996, p. 253). de Man and Roijakkers (2009) state that relational risk is perceived as a threat that a firm will behave opportunistically and deliberately harm its partner's interests. Partners in alliances usually have hidden agendas, which again makes it challenging to cooperate in an alliance (Das & Teng, 2001).

Performance risk is the perceived chance that factors such as market uncertainty, competition, and governmental regulation may have negative effects on alliance results (de Man & Roijakkers, 2009, p. 77). Clearly, there will be always a risk that is not contingent upon how good the cooperation between partners is. On the other side, such alliances share risk, which is also a part of performance risk. What can reduce performance risks in such alliances is e.g. R&D investments, jointly bidding for large projects and entering new markets.

The distinction between relational risks and performance risk is crucial (Das & Teng, 2001). As de Man and Roijakkers (2009, p. 76) propose, a high relational risk and a low performance risk require strict alliance control, while in the reverse situation the alliance will fare better under trust-based governance. de Man and Roijakkers (2009) continue that when both elements of risk are high, control and trust are complementary.

Trust

According to Alm et al. (2013) trust is not necessarily between two persons; it can also be a trust chain. In the trust chain there are several actors that have to trust each other, e.g. A needs to trust B, which then has to firmly believe in C, which has trust D (Alm et al., 2013). This shows that there is dependence throughout the whole chain when one actor could act without taking into consideration what others have been doing in such a trust chain. To follow Alm et al. (2013), results in the trust chain can be achieved slowly because of the input from several parties. Such a project typically requires contributions from different groups of professionals (Alm et al., 2013). In this chapter, we consider MaaS as an example of a trust chain.

Trust is the phenomenon that exists on personal, organizational, interorganizational, and international levels (Ring & Van de Ven, 1992; Sydow, 1998). Trust in cooperative relationships is effective in reducing concerns about opportunistic behavior. It also makes for better integration between the partners, and reduces the need for formal contracts (Das & Teng, 2001). Building trust in platforms is essential; this is typically done through rating systems, payment mechanisms, or insurance. In the absence of trust, the players on the platform have to make a leap of faith (Yoffie et al.,). There are two categories of trust in strategic alliances; goodwill trust and competence trust.

Goodwill trust is about good faith, good intentions, and integrity exercised between partners (Das & Teng, 2001). With a reputation for goodwill trust, it is easier to cooperate, rather than partners believing that the firm will behave opportunistically in the alliance or partnership. Langfield-Smith (2008) states that goodwill trust can evolve over time based on different interests, can build up individual and team-based trust, and at the same time can create institutional trust to optimally resolve possible disputes. Thus, according to Das and Teng (2001, p. 257), a firm's goodwill trust in its partner firm reduces its perceived relational risk in an alliance, but not its perceived performance risk.

Competence trust is based on the various resources and capabilities of a firm (Das & Teng, 2001). Resources may include capital, human resources, physical properties, market power, technology, etc. Jiang et al. (2015) state that competence trust is the belief of one partner that another partner has enough resources and competences to accomplish agreed tasks in the alliance. These resources and capabilities provide a basis for the competence or expertise that is needed in alliances or partnerships. Those firms that have been successful in previous alliances have a reputation for competence, and thus are more sought after to establish further cooperation. Competence is the factor that suggests a high probability of getting things accomplished, and thus lowering performance risk. Therefore, according to Das and Teng (2001, p. 258), a firm's competence trust in its cooperation reduces its perceived performance risk, but not its perceived relational risk.

Control

Besides trust, control is another essential factor in strategic alliances. In alliances, control can be achieved through governance structures, contractual specifications, managerial arrangements, and other more informal mechanisms (Das & Teng, 2001). As Das and Teng (2001, p. 258) state, "control in alliances is of two types – controlling the partner and controlling the alliance per se". However, because of complexities in managing alliances, control mechanisms are also conducive to coordination and learning. Effective control thus becomes important for alliance performance (Das & Teng, 2001). Control may also have negative effects on the alliance. As Das and Teng (2001, p. 258), citing Provan and Skinner, show, "dealers' opportunistic behaviour is positively related to supplier control over dealers' decisions".

The control literature proposes two approaches to control: formal and informal, which in turn have the following modes as for formal control – behavior and output, and for informal control – social control (see e.g., Ouchi, 1979; Das & Teng, 2001; Langfield-Smith, 2008).

Behavioral control is also called process control, since it focuses on the process that turns appropriate behavior into desirable output (Das & Teng, 2001). However, managers in the alliances may encounter difficulties in measuring the outcomes of opportunistic behavior and relational conflicts in a precise and objective manner.

Output control is results-oriented and what makes it difficult to measure behavior, but at the same time it is possible to measure the product or service that comes out. The firm's set of management goals may provide the firm's own "output" control mechanism. Das and Teng (2001) state that output control helps to direct the attention of alliance managers to key performance measures.

Social control focuses on developing shared values, beliefs, and goals among members so that appropriate behavior will be reinforced and rewarded (Ouchi, 1979). According to Das and Teng (2001), in strategic alliances social control is often used as it is through a socialization and consensus-making process that members become more committed to the organization.

Interplay between risk, trust, and control

According to Das and Teng (2001), not only does control influence trust in an alliance, but trust also affects the effectiveness of control. To implement control in the organization requires a certain level of trust (Creed & Miles, 1996; Das & Teng, 1998). In that case social control functions best when there is a relatively high level of trust between different partners. On the other side, behavior control and output control also work better in the presence of trust between partners. In addition, Vryza and Fryxell (1997) found that trust makes control mechanisms more effective. Lack of a certain level of trust can lead to a lack of cooperation between different partners (Das & Teng, 2001). That is to say, following Das and Teng (2001), that goodwill trust and competence trust enhance the effectiveness of all control modes (behavior, output, and social) in an alliance.

Das and Teng (2001), Cannon et al. (2000), and Creed and Miles (1996) all claim that trust and control can *individually* reduce risk, but also point out that *together* trust and control can lower the risk for firms in alliances. It is important to have both trust and control mechanisms that can minimize the risk in strategic alliances. If this is not the case, the risk will increase and the cooperation between the various partners will be undermined. This may cause the goal of the strategic alliance to become unattainable and in the worst case, the alliance may be dissolved.

Partners in alliances are exposed to both relationship risk and performance risk. According to Das and Teng (2001), there is an upper limit to how much risk a partner can carry in an alliance. If the level of risk in an alliance is too high, the various partners will have to rely on trust and control to reduce the risk.

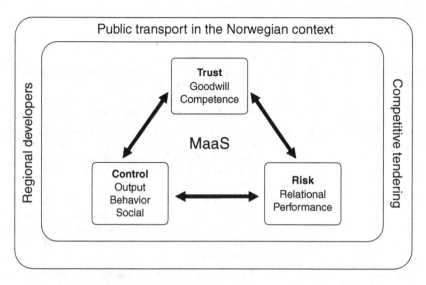

Figure 3.1 The framework for analyzing trust, control, and risk in MaaS alliances as applies to the Norwegian context for public passenger transport. Adapted from Das and Teng (2001)

It is important to emphasize the Norwegian context as it may present a different setting relative to other MaaS projects. In Norway, it is the public regional developers (hereafter referred to as "developers") that deal with tenders submitted for public passenger transport. By combining the Norwegian context with empirical evidence on the interplay between trust, control, and risk, we seek a better understanding of how a MaaS alliance can function in such a setting and compare our findings with those in the existing literature. Figure 3.1 will serve as our analysis tool.

Empirical data

When addressing the interplay between trust, control, and risk in MaaS alliances, in practice we make use of empirical data from the Norwegian public passenger transport industry based on the theoretical framework presented in Figure 3.1. We want to study which forms of control are most appropriate for use in different types of alliances and at the same time reveal which forms of trust and risk such strategic alliances lead to.

The criteria for selecting organizations for our study were 1) that the company must be in a strategic MaaS alliance and 2) that the company must have started or will develop a pilot project applying MaaS. By the use of these criteria we arrived at the four organizations listed in Table 3.1. Because there are relatively few ongoing projects, we were able to consult the main

Table 3.1 Description of the selected organizations

Organization	Role of organization	Description of MaaS project
Nordland county	Developer	A cooperation of MaaS in the city of Bodø scheduled to be up and running by 2023. Partners are Nordland county, Avinor (airport owner), Telenor (digital communication service provider) and Bodø municipality.
Institute of Transport Economics	Researcher	A national center for research in transport and communications with responsibility for promoting research results relevant for businesses and society in Norway. This institute has conducted several R&D studies on MaaS solutions.
Ruter AS	Developer	Responsible for planning, coordination, procurement, and promotion of public transport in the region around the capital of Oslo. They have an ongoing MaaS project aiming to reduce the use of private cars. Ruter is publicly owned.
Kolumbus	Developer	A supplier of mobility services with responsibility for major parts of public transport in Rogaland county. The aim is to make transport solutions that enable reduced use of private cars. Kolumbus is publicly owned.

representatives of actors involved in the MaaS solutions in the Norwegian context, i.e. public authorities in charge for public transport services, an R&D organization with responsibility for transport service analysis, and the technical developers of MaaS solutions responsible for ongoing MaaS projects in Norway. These selected cases exemplify the main actors in the business model of the sharing economy responsible for the rules and regulations of the platform, as Parente et al. (2018, p. 54) state "sharing economy firms function as an interface connecting different groups of users […] that interact accordingly to certain 'rules' and guidelines".

Our interviewees are people with extensive networks and part of the process of developing a MaaS solution. Based on the data we gather, we contemplate how trust, control, and risk appear in various MaaS alliances in the Norwegian context.

The criteria for selecting the informant within an organization was that he/she must have a significant role or particularly good insight into the strategic alliance. Interviews were carried out either face-to-face or by telephone depending on what was most convenient given the time and availability of the informant. The interviews were completed over a period of six weeks in the first part of 2019. Details on the type and duration of the interviews with the informants in the four organizations are given in Table 3.2.

When gathering the primary data we applied a semi-structured approach with an interview guide. This enabled us both to gather the same type of

Table 3.2 Details on the informants

Informant	Organization	Interview approach	Duration of interview
Informant 1	Nordland county	Personal interview	1h 18 min
Informant 2	Institute of Transport Economics	Telephone interview	38 min
Informant 3	Ruter	Telephone interview	43 min
Informant 4	Kolumbus	Telephone interview	1h 24 min

basic information from all interviewees by referring to the overall interview guide and to allow for freedom to follow up on relevant topics and statements. The interviews were transcribed shortly after the completion of the interview to ensure that the responses were fresh in mind. Finally, the transcribed text was returned to the respondents for approval and comments on intended meanings were incorporated.

The interviews were recorded, which means that the original data material can be accessed. Ethical aspects of the research design were approved by the Norwegian Centre for Research Data. Our data sets were anonymized and deleted after completion of the study. Our theoretical framework is based on the existing literature evolving around the factors of trust, control, and risk in strategic alliances and thereby addresses the topics relevant for the study. We therefore contend that the necessary steps were indeed taken to ensure both reliability and validity.

Interplay between trust, control, and risk in non-equity sharing alliances

In this section we will apply our empirical findings to the theoretical framework to discuss the overall research question of explaining the role of trust, control, and risk in MaaS alliances using empirical data from the Norwegian context. In the analysis we use the framework in Figure 3.1 building on the theory as a basis for discussing the different relationships. We will address the three pillars of Figure 3.1 by starting with the relationship between trust and control, then trust and risk, and control and risk. Finally, we address the overall question of how trust and control can lead to reduced risk in non-equity alliances within this context.

Control in relation to trust

In a MaaS alliance developers need to have contracts in place due to the large number of actors cooperating in the public transport market. The MaaS developers must have contracts as a support, and they admit that these are quite rigid and encourage no flexibility in behavior. Yes this does not mean that they do not pay attention to trust. Social control is of particular importance for building trust in both competence and goodwill, perhaps because this is an early phase or start-up phase. This is also because developers know that trust in each other in the alliance is critical to make the project work. Developers must have trust in their alliance partners when it comes to sharing sensitive data, how this is treated and used, and in order to obtain the strategic objectives set for the alliance.

There are limits to how informative and specific a contract can be and Informant 4 from Kolombus explained that they were participating in breakfasts at partners premises to build trust and at the same time learn from them. From our empirical evidence we see that developers are aware that the level of control is high and that they continuously aim to increase trust between their project partners. They also state that this is how the process has to be; start with rigid contracts and then build trust in the relationship. This could have to do with the Norwegian context, because when the MaaS solution is introduced in new regions the developers cannot automatically choose partners previously involved in pilot projects. There has to be a round of competitive tendering to set the stage for a situation in which the firms they have cooperated with earlier may be outbid by other firms.

Trust in relation to risk

According to Lui and Ngo (2004), trust can be seen as an important element in the total assessment of perceived risk. It is argued that competence trust and other forms for trust are closely connected to different types of risk in non-equity alliances. It was particularly clear that competence trust influenced perceived performance risk and that goodwill risk will influence perceived relational risk (Lui & Ngo, 2004).

In the non-equity alliances studied there was generally a high degree of competence trust and goodwill trust. The high level of competence trust was in this case attributable to the partners' belief that the MaaS developer had everything necessary for the successful completion of the MaaS project. Competence trust may also be related to the procurement arrangements of competitive tendering. In these well specified tenders there are a number of criteria that must be fulfilled by the cooperating organizations and it is therefore important for the MaaS developers to have competence trust in all participants that they have the skill and resources to fulfil the work assignments given in the contracts. This expectation is fully in line with the definition of competence trust proposed by Jiang et al. (2015). Consequently, the high degree of competence trust we observed in the MaaS alliances will contribute to reducing the level of performance risk.

Our results also show that goodwill trust in non-equity alliances can be regarded as high. This high level differs from the perception by Das and Teng (2001) that goodwill trust is normally not so important in such alliances. Our respondents argue that goodwill trust is needed for the different organizations to have control over the sharing and treatment of sensitive data. It is important to have this type of trust since it would otherwise be difficult to have a complete overview of how each of the partners in the alliance handles these data. Since the different actors depend on having goodwill trust in this situation, a high level of trust would contribute to reducing the level of relational risk.

Risk in relation to control

It is generally accepted that social control and behavioral control could contribute to reducing the level of relational risk in an alliance, while output control and social control could contribute to reducing performance risk. If goodwill trust is unchanged and it is accepted as having only a low level of relational risk, there will be a need for compensation through stricter behavioral and social control. If, on the other hand, competence trust is at a fixed level and a low level of performance risk is accepted, then there will be a need to compensate with a higher level of output control and social control in the alliance (Das & Teng, 2001).

Our respondents stated that output control in non-equity alliances should be regarded as high. Again, this is a finding that can be related to the context of competitive tendering. These procurement contracts will have qualitative and quantitative requirements that various partners must fulfil to engage in a contract. By using these contracts it is difficult to measure the behavior of the various organizations, but the contracts may provide standards for the measurement of output. Output is here understood as whether the organizations comply with the terms and deliverables specified in the contracts. Using such a contract entails rules and recommendations that will contribute to reducing the risk of the contract specifications not being met. For this reason we would argue that our data set supports the view that output control in such an alliance will contribute to reducing the performance risk.

Moreover, our findings demonstrate that social control in this case should be regarded as moderate. This differs to some extent from the claim by Das and Teng (2001) that social control in such alliances should be regarded as high. In our data set social control often assumed the form of the partners in the alliance making personal visits to each other. This could be meetings intended to build social control by means of social initiatives, frequent meetings, and dialogue. We defined social control as moderate in this situation because MaaS developers use these interactions as a way to build trust between partners, but not as a control mechanism. Hence, we do not assess the social control as high. As argued by Das and Teng (2001), social control could contribute to reducing both performance and relational risk. According to our data this effect is at a moderate level.

Our data indicates that behavior control should be considered as low in this type of alliances. Our results thereby deviate from those of Das and Teng (2001) arguing that behavior control is moderate in non-equity alliances. In MaaS projects within the Norwegian context there is a clear perception that all partners have a high level of trust in contracts. While it is difficult to measure the behavior of each of the partners, there are great opportunities for measuring the output of the agreements concluded. Specifically, it would be difficult to measure and review the behavior of partners if the organizations are located in different geographical regions. Consequently, we argue that behavioral control should be regarded as low in this setting. This implies that behavioral control does not contribute to reducing the level of relational risk between partners, but rather that the opposite may be the case.

Reducing risk by trust and control in non-equity sharing alliances

In the previous sections we discussed what our respondents revealed about the interplay between trust, control, and risk in non-equity alliances. These findings are summarized in Table 3.3. Table 3.3 is an adapted version of the framework developed by Das and Teng (2001). While Das and Teng (2001) in their original framework focused on reduction of risk by mechanisms of trust and control only in strategic alliances, our framework in Table 3.3 addresses to a larger extent purely non-equity alliances of MaaS solutions. The four cells in Table 3.3 where our results deviate from the original framework by Das and Teng (2001) are presented in bold face and italics. In the following we comment specifically on these combinations of different types of trust and control.

Let us first address the cell in Table 3.3 addressing goodwill trust and behavioral control. Goodwill trust can, according to Das and Teng (2001), contribute to influencing relational risk, but performance risk will remain high because it cannot be addressed by goodwill trust and behavioral control. The same is found for behavioral control, which can contribute to reducing relational risk. Our findings show that goodwill trust in non-equity alliances can be regarded as high, while this relationship is low for behavioral control. Since both factors could contribute to reduced relational risk, a combination of high degree of goodwill trust and low degree of behavioral control leads to a total assessment

Table 3.3 Risk reduction through trust and control in non-equity alliances. Combinations deviating from the original model by Das and Teng (2001) is highlighted with bold face and italics

	Behavior control	*Output control*	*Social control*
Goodwill trust	***moderate*** relational risk *high* performance risk	moderate relational risk moderate performance risk	low relational risk **high** performance risk
Competence trust	**high** relational risk *moderate* performance risk	high relational risk low performance risk	**high** relational risk low performance risk

of the impact of relational control being moderate. In our case the performance risk is also high and this is a consequence of goodwill trust and behavioral control having limited influence on the performance risk.

Then the next cell below in Table 3.3 contains a combination of competence trust and behavioral control. Das and Teng (2001) argue in the original framework that the degree of competence trust in a strategical alliance can contribute to reducing performance risk while having no influence on relational risk. Our findings indicate that in non-equity MaaS alliances there is a high degree of competence trust. The interplay of competence trust with the low degree of behavioral control leads to a moderate influence on performance risk. Behavioral control would in this situation contribute to reducing relational risk, but competence risk has no influence on this type of risk. By contrast our respondents were of the opinion that behavioral control should be regarded as low and we argue for setting this at a high level for MaaS alliances in Norway.

Then we can focus on the combination of output control and goodwill trust in Table 3.3. Das and Teng (2001) argue in the original framework that output control can reduce performance risk. Our findings argue for both a high level of output control and goodwill trust. However, since the two factors only reduce one of the types of risk in a MaaS project, we argue that overall both forms of risk should be regarded as moderate.

Our findings demonstrate that the combination of competence trust and output control should be regarded as high in non-equity alliances. Das and Teng (2001) argue that both competence trust and output control could contribute to reducing the level of performance risk, but with little effect on relational risk. Consequently, a high level of these two factors would lead to the performance risk among actors in this context of being low, while the relational risk would be high.

At the top right in Table 3.3 we have the combination of social control and goodwill. Our findings indicate that for non-equity alliances in the MaaS context social control should be regarded as moderate while goodwill trust is high. Das and Teng (2001) argue that social control can reduce the levels of both relational risk and performance risk. We have argued that goodwill trust could reduce relational risk, but not performance risk. Hence, the moderate degree of social control in combination with the high degree of goodwill trust leads to the relational risk being perceived as low while the performance risk is perceived as high.

The last combination in Table 3.3 addresses the combination of social control and competence trust. We saw in our findings that social control had a moderate influence in non-equity alliances, while competence trust was regarded as high. Das and Teng (2001) argue that social control can reduce both types of risk, while competence trust only influences performance risk. A moderate degree of social control in combination with a high degree of competence trust will in our context lead to a high relational risk and a low performance risk.

Conclusions and implications

In this chapter, we showed how trust, control and risk can function in strategic alliances in platform organizations, and in particular in the non-equity alliances of MaaS solutions. We discussed this interplay in the Norwegian context with special reference to publicly owned regional developers initiating projects and obliged to follow the rules and regulations pertaining to the development of MaaS projects. In addition, these regional developers have social responsibility for the public transport sector in the respective regions. In conducting our study we sought a better understanding of trust, control, and risk in the Norwegian MaaS alliances as platform organizations and showed that with such interplay between trust, control, and risk MaaS solutions can contribute to increased sustainability awareness in passenger transport.

Our empirical analysis showed that trust, control, and risk in non-equity alliances yield a more nuanced picture when it comes to the Norwegian context. We show that goodwill trust is quite important in such alliances since the EU General Data Protection Regulation (GDPR) is a significant feature when it comes to developing MaaS projects in Norway. The GDPR is not necessarily what immediately comes to mind with regard to goodwill trust. However, it is quite important; developers do need to have trust that other actors in non-equity alliances can handle personal data in a secure and proper way. Moreover, our study showed that the Norwegian context is characterized by behavior control being lower than that discussed by Das and Teng (2001). This is attributable to the fact that Norwegian MaaS alliances involve numerous actors, which makes it challenging to control the behavior of all parties. We also established that social control was regarded as moderate in comparison to that reported by Das and Teng (2001) since Norwegian MaaS solutions used it not as a control mechanism, but as a trust-builder during the start-up period of the project. Our findings therefore also reveal a change in risk reduction through trust and control.

Our empirical data showed that since the Norwegian context differs from those of other countries, the development of MaaS in Norway is more complex. Developers of MaaS are nowadays obliged to follow the procedures of competitive tendering. As some of our informants pointed out, this may halt the innovation process by not involving new and smaller actors operating in the transport sector unable to compete against big firms. Nevertheless, all actors involved are aware of these procedures and are used to taking part in them. Thus, competitive tendering makes it possible for every firm to participate and to compete under the same conditions. What also emerges from our study is that MaaS developers have social responsibility in connection with environmental protection, better health, and financial sustainability, and thus influencing sustainable development awareness by changing consumer habits and practices. Their main task is not to make a profit, but to provide the Norwegian population with reasonable transportation options. It would have been interesting to study the consequences if MaaS projects in Norway had been implemented only by private actors.

Our empirical findings indicate that for MaaS projects in the Norwegian context, i.e., for developers, it is crucial to have a high degree of control in the form of contracts. This enables them to reduce the risks for all actors involved in the project. We also found that trust is the critical success factor for Norwegian MaaS projects to operate optimally. On the one hand this can be explained by a willingness to decrease the risk, but at the same time it is also due to the fact that it is of the utmost importance for actors to avoid abusing the sensitive personal data that developers in MaaS alliances do not always control. The risk in such non-equity alliances varies. However, these alliances can deal with high risks because it costs less and actors trust that developers have the competence, resources, and capabilities to accomplish such an extensive project.

The interplay between trust, control, and risk in the Norwegian MaaS alliances affords a better understanding of trust, control, and risk. In particular, MaaS developers planning to implement a MaaS project can get a more nuanced picture of how such alliances can function and what kind of factors are the most important in the start-up period. As a consequence, the knowledge about the relationships between trust, control, and risk in this context will produce better projects and thereby deliver better value for society. If these three aspects are not understood, then projects could fail and passengers will suffer and so also the businesses since people will not be able to commute or customers arrive on time. In the broader perspective, this knowledge specifically addresses the UN Sustainable Development Goals related to providing sustainable infrastructure and managing sustainable cities (e.g., goals 9 and 11). In our study we contribute to the research on platform organizations as non-equity alliances in the public transport sector by considering the Norwegian context consisting largely of public sector actors rather than of private actors.

Regarding future research, opportunities for studying MaaS alliances abound. It would be useful to study how the project functions after being in use for some period of time. It would be worth considering how the knowledge connected to the interplay between trust, control, and risk developed during the project. It would also be useful to shed light on how different actors experience trust, control, and risk in such alliances after being in operation for some time. In addition, it would be appropriate to explore how MaaS projects once developed operate in small and big cities. As we have shown, in Norway, MaaS projects are driven by public actors, yet it would also have be relevant to study how such projects can function with developers from the private sector and as a follow up, to compare MaaS projects implemented in Norway with projects e.g. in Sweden, where the transport sector is privatized within MaaS development.

Notes

1 https://www.lexico.com/en/definition/sharing_economy.
2 For more information on the SDGs we refer readers to https://sustainabledevelopment. un.org/sdgs.

References

Aarhaug, J. (2017). Discussing MaaS and its possibilities in Norwegian city regions. TØI Report: 1578/2017. Oslo, Institute of Transport Economics. Available at: www.toi.no/getfile.php?mmfileid=45879.

Alm, K., Andersen, E.S., & Kvalnes, Ø. (2013). Tillit i prosjekter. *Magma, 16*(3), 26–33. Available at www.magma.no/tillit-i-prosjekter.

Bierly, P.E., & Coombs, J.E. (2004). Equity alliances stages of product development, and alliance instability. *Journal of Engineering and Technology Management, 21*(3), 191–214. doi: https://doi.org/10.1016/j.jengtecman.2004.05.001.

Cannon, J.P., Achrol, R.S., & Gundlach, G.T. (2000). Contracts, norms, and plural form governance. *Journal of the Academy of Marketing Science, 28*(2), 180–194. doi: 10.1177/0092070300282001.

Creed, W.E.D., & Miles, R.E. (1996). Trust in organizations: A conceptual framework. In. In R.M. Kramer & T.R. Tyler (eds.). *Trust in organizations: Frontiers of theory and research.* London: Sage, pp. 16–39.

Das, T.K., & Teng, B. (1996). Risk types and inter-firm alliance structures. *Journal of Management Studies, 33*, 827–843.

Das, T.K., & Teng, B.S. (1998). Between trust and control: Developing confidence in partner cooperation in alliances. *Academy of Management Review, 23*(3), 491–512.

Das, T.K., & Teng, B.S. (1999). Managing risks in strategic alliances. *The Academy of Management Executive, 13*(4), 50–62.

Das, T.K., & Teng, B.S. (2001). Trust, control, and risk in strategic alliances: An integrated framework. *Organization Studies, 22*(2), 251–283.

de Man, A.-P., & Roijakkers, N. (2009). Alliance governance: Balancing control and trust in dealing with risk. *Long Range Planning, 42*, 75–95.

Goodall, W., Dovey Fishman, T., Bornstein, J., & Bonthron, B. (2017). The rise of mobility as a service: Reshaping how urbanites get around. *Deloitte Review, 20*, 111–129.

Haugland, S.A. (2004). *Samarbeid, allianser og nettverk.* Oslo: Universitetsforlaget.

Heinrichs, H. (2013). Sharing economy: A potential new pathway to sustainability. *Gaia, 22*(4), 228–231.

Hensher, D.A. (2017). Future bus transport contracts under a mobility as a service (MaaS) regime in the digital age: Are they likely to change? *Transportation Research, 98*, 86–96. doi: http://dx.doi.org/10.1016/j.tra.2017.02.006.

Jiang, X., Jiang, F., Cai, X., & Liu, H. (2015). How does trust affect alliance performance?: The mediating role of resource sharing. *Industrial Marketing Management, 45*, 128–138.

Johnson, G., Whittington, R., Scholes, K., Angwin, D., & Regnér, P. (2017). *Exploring strategy text and cases.* Harlow: Pearson.

Kornberger, M., Pflueger, D., & Mouritsen, J. (2017). Evaluative infrastructures: Accounting for platform organization. *Accounting, Organizations and Society, 60*, 79–95. doi: http://dx.doi.org/10.1016/j.aos.2017.05.002.

Langfield-Smith, K. (2008). The relations between transactional characteristics, trust and risk in the start-up phase of a collaborative alliance. *Management Accounting Research, 19*, 344–364.

Lui, S.S., & Ngo, H.-Y. (2004). The role of trust and contractual safeguards on cooperation in non-equity alliances. *Journal of Management, 30*(4), 471–485. doi: 10.1016/j.jm.2004.02.002.

Mulley, C., Nelson, J.D., & Wright, S. (2018). Community transport meets mobility as a service: On the road to a new a flexible future. *Research in Transportation Economics, 69*, 583–591.

Ouchi, W.G. (1979). A conceptual framework for the design of organizational control mechanisms. *Management Science, 25*, 833–848.

Parente, R.C., Geleilate, J.-M.G., & Rong, K. (2018). The sharing economy globalization phenomenon: A research agenda. *Journal of International Management, 24*, 52–64.

Ring, P.S., & Van de Ven, A.H. (1992). Structuring cooperative relationships between organizations. *Strategic Management Journal, 13*, 483–498.

Schumacher, C. (2006). Trust – A source of success in strategic alliances?. *Schmalenbach Business Review: ZFBF, 58*(3), 259–278.

Strømmen-Bakhtiar, A., & Vinogradov, E. (2019). The effects of Airbnb on hotels in Norway. *Society and Economy, 41*(1), 87–105.

Sydow, J. (1998). Understanding the constitution of interorganizational trust. In C. Lane & R. Bachmann (eds.). *Trust within and between organizations: Conceptual issues and empirical applications*. New York: Oxford University, pp. 31–63.

The Economist. (2016). It starts with a single app. *The Economist*, 29.09.2016. Available at: www.economist.com/international/2016/09/29/it-starts-with-a-single-app.

Vryza, M., & Fryxell, G.E. (1997). *The interaction of trust and control mechanisms in the management of successful international joint ventures*. Paper presented at the annual meeting of the Academy of Management, Boston.

Yoffie, D.B., Gawer, A., & Cusumano, M.A. (2019). Social platforms: A study of more than 250 platforms reveals why most fail. *Harvard Business Review*, 29 May 2019.

4 The effect of Airbnb on rents and house prices in Norway

Abbas Strømmen-Bakhtiar and Evgueni Vinogradov

Introduction

The relatively recent rapid worldwide expansion of the short-term letting platforms such as Airbnb has started a heated discussion on the effects of these companies on house prices and the private and commercial rental markets. Specifically, it is opined that the lower transaction costs and higher rental rates are fueling speculation in the housing market (Boone, 2018; Segú, 2018; Wachsmuth & Weisler, 2017). Those that until the advent of these platforms have been averse to speculating in the real estate market, see their risks reduced. They can now buy an extra apartment or a house in the belief that Airbnb and the like can provide them with a venue to generate much higher rents fees at a lower transaction cost than previously possible. The housing advocates have become increasingly concerned that landlords use the Airbnb services to let their units to tourists and other visitors instead of renting them to locals, thereby causing a shortage of rental units, and subsequently driving-up rent rates (Barron, Kung & Proserpio, 2018; Rosenberg, 2018).

Homeownership varies from country to country. For example, in Europe, we see Romania at the top of the list with 96% home ownership while Switzerland with 42% finds itself at the bottom (Statista, 2016). Norway, with 77.6% is above average (Statistics Norway-SSB, 2016).

For most people, buying a house represents one of the major investments of their life. A house is not only a place where one lives, but it can also be a source of income or be used as collateral for loans. As such people are concerned with the value of their investment in housing and anything that can positively affect their investment is welcomed. This is not so for those who are renting.

People are not the only ones concerned with house prices. Governments both at the national and local level are also concerned with house prices since housing's influence on the economy extends beyond its direct contribution. Careful analysis reveals that housing also influences the level of consumer spending. When housing wealth increases, consumers spend more. Indeed, they spend even more freely when capital gains from home sales and home equity borrowing escalate in tandem with rising home values (Belsky & Prakken, 2004). While rising house prices can on a moderate level have a positive effect on the economy by for example contributing to increasing activities in construction sector employment and home appliances sales, it can have a negative effect on rents.

These discussions have resulted in intervention by some cities and municipal authorities in the rental markets. For example, In May 2016, Berlin started implementing a law that was passed in 2014 with a two-year grace period, restricting private property rentals through Airbnb and similar platforms. The law is meant to stop the tremendous rise in the rents which, between 2009 and 2014, had risen by 56% (France-Presse, 2016). In another move, the local authorities in London and Amsterdam (December 2016) forced Airbnb to take on "the responsibility of policing limits on the number of days per year a full unit can be let through its system, making it the first short-term rental company to cut such a deal" (Woolf, 2016). Recently the Japanese government began considering laws to restrict the size of the rooms and the minimum stay to one week (Wakatsuki & Ripley, 2016).

Airbnb is also expanding rapidly and causing a considerable problem. According to the chairperson of Visit Svalbard (tourist information office), in 2017, 20% of all beds in the area were listed on Airbnb (Svalbardposten, 2017). By the beginning of 2018, there has been no sign of the Airbnb growth flattening out. Now local employees find it difficult to find affordable rental accommodations, forcing some to resign and return to the mainland (Svalbardposten, 2018).

Of course, Airbnb, as the largest letting platform in the world, disputes these allegations, arguing that majority of units that are announced on its platform would have stayed empty had it not been for Airbnb. However, considering the scarcity of available data, it has been difficult to ascertain to what degree these claims and counterclaims are correct. This paper tries to address these concerns.

Literature review

Airbnb is a platform-based business model, popularly referred to as the "sharing economy". Botsman and Rogers (2010, pp. 159–160) define sharing economy broadly as – "traditional sharing, bartering, lending, trading, renting, gifting, and swapping, redefined through technology and peer communities", while the Ministry of Local Government and Regional Development (CMD) defines sharing economy as "coupling between individuals and/or legal entities through digital platforms that facilitate the provision of services and/ or sharing of assets/property, resources, expertise or capital without transferring ownership rights" (Kartlegging av delingsøkonomien i Norge, 2016).

The sharing economy is a rental/services business model with some innovations. These innovations have been around three elements of the business model: (1) the platform (market), (2) the reputation system (trust), and (3) flexibility (time). At the heart of this business model, we find the platform, which using telecommunication technologies such as the location-based services, brings the lender/service provider and the renter/consumer together. The location-based services have considerably reduced the cost of locating providers and consumers. However, conducting transactions between strangers require a high degree of trust. In impersonal markets, especially the digital ones, trust is hard to establish. The reputation system, where users of the platform (providers and consumers) rate each other seems to have, solved this problem. Also, all monetary transactions are performed via Airbnb and associated credit cards further reducing risks for users.

The next innovation is in time flexibility around the duration of the rental agreement. The renting duration and hence cost has always been connected to the costs of locating customers and the administration costs. These considerations had always limited the duration to an optimal minimum time. For example, the minimum duration for renting cars was set to one day, or for hotels to one night. The technology has reduced the costs of finding lenders/renters and administration costs, thereby allowing a marked reduction in lending time. This reduction in minimum lending-time has made it possible for "people to turn otherwise unproductive assets into producing ones" (Carter, 2015, p. 8).

In 2007, Brian Chesky and Joe Gebbia founded the "Airbed & Breakfast" the predecessor of Airbnb. In 2008 Nathan Blecharczyk joined the two, and in 2009, the name was changed to Airbnb. By 2010, the venture capital money was pouring in to finance Airbnb's rapid expansion across the globe. Today, Airbnb is present in 191 countries and covers 34,000 cities worldwide with the highest growth present in traditional tourist destinations such as Paris, London, New York, Rome, and the like (Figure 4.1). The lack of regulations, ease of access to the market and low transaction costs have been the main facilitators of expansion of Airbnb in these countries.

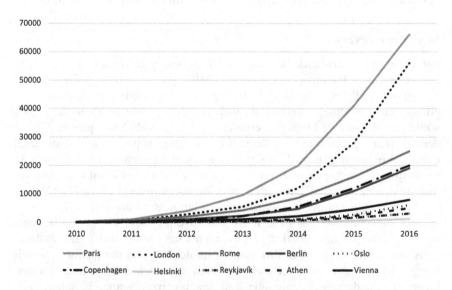

Figure 4.1 Airbnb growth in ten selected cities around the world 2010–2016.
Source: Airdna (2018).

Factors affecting house prices

Factors affecting house prices can be divided into national and local factors. National factors such as interest rate, credit and national regulations affect house prices uniformly across the country, while local factors such as land prices, tourism, employment, demography, crime, local town planning regulations, and infrastructure affect house prices locally and can vary from town to town and from region to region (Beltratti & Morana, 2010; Capozza, Hendershott, Mack & Mayer, 2002; Girouard, Kennedy, Van Den Noord & André, 2006; Tsatsaronis & Zhu, 2004). These differences can be seen through plotting the house prices for various towns and cities. If they rise and fall uniformly, then on average, it is national factors that play a larger role than local factors.

For example, looking at the Norwegian house price movement for a ten-year period (Figure 4.1), one sees that house prices across the country follow the same pattern. Except for places, such as "Agder and Rogaland" and "Vestlandet" (regions in Norway) where the fall in oil prices affected the oil-related industries.

Studies (Gallin, 2008; Himmelberg, Mayer & Sinai, 2005) have shown that there is a relatively strong connection between house prices and rents. As house prices increase, so do the rents, although not always at the same rate. This connection is referred to as the price-to-rent ratio. This connection is also mentioned by Jacobsen and Naug (2005) who in addition to interest rates, mention other factors such as housing construction costs, unemployment, and household income.

In this study it is is argued that Airbnb is another important factor that should be included in the list of factors affecting house prices. Airbnb can influence

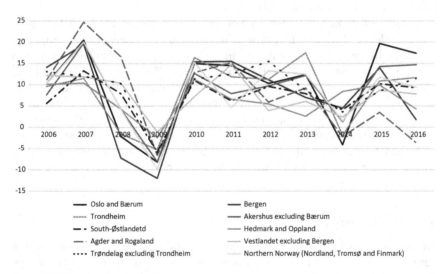

Figure 4.2 House prices over time.
Source: "Prisindeks for brukte boliger. Statistikkbanken," (2018).

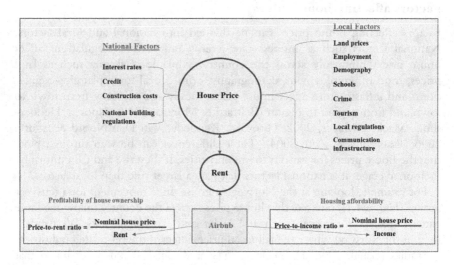

Figure 4.3 The factors affecting house prices and rents.

house prices through an increase in rental income. As can be seen in Figure 4.2, this increase in rental income affects house prices through increased profitability of house ownership by reducing the price-to-rent ratio (increasing rents), while increasing housing affordability through increasing general income. The increase in profitability of house ownership and housing affordability directly affect house prices (see Figure 4.3). This also allows people with higher income to buy second houses to engage in the rental business.

A study of Airbnb activities in London by Quattrone et al. (2016) "provided evidence that, when treating Airbnb listings homogeneously, properties are more likely to be concentrated in tech-savvy and well-to-do areas with young renters." Another study this time, of New York city, by Sheppard and Udell (2016), using a hedonic model, showed that a doubling of Airbnb listing was associated with 6% to 11% increase in house prices while using a difference-in-difference approach showed an increase of 31%. Another study by Barron, Kung and Proserpio (2017), using a comprehensive dataset of Airbnb listings from the entire United States, found that a 10% increase in Airbnb listing leads to 0.42% increase in rents and a 0.76% increase in housing prices.

The case of Norway

Norway is a small country with a population of 5.29 million. Its capital, the country's largest city, has a population of close to a million, followed by Bergen (pop. 254,000), Stavanger (pop. 220,000), Trondheim (pop. 180,000), and Drammen (pop. 116,000).

Table 4.1 Households by type of ownership and type of building, by overcrowding, the number and percentage

	2015	
	N	*Percent*
Households, self-ownership	1,457,979	63.2
Households, Housing associations	329,120	14.3
Households, renters	521,290	22.6
Households in detached houses	1,118,983	48.5
Households in apartments	544,064	23.6
Persons that live in cramped conditions, few rooms	541,968	10.7
Children and young people (0–19 years old) that live in cramped conditions, few rooms	228,808	18.3

Source: Statistics Norway-SSB (2016).

Norway is one of a few countries in the world where the majority of the population own their homes. According to Statistics Norway-SSB (2016), 77.5% of the population own their homes, with 48% of those owning a detached house (Table 4.1).

That leaves 22.6% of the population, or 521,290 people, that have to live in rental accommodation, the majority (close to 65%) of which receive social help and housing allowance ("Boforhold, registerbasert, 2015," 2016). Overall, 60% of all families at the lower income levels, rent. Students who do not live with their parents, compose another segment that lives in rented accommodations. This means that any changes in rental accommodation availability will disproportionately affect the economically weak.

The distribution of the renters varies across the country, with the majority, being concentrated in the large cities. For example, shares of households on the rental market in Oslo, Trondheim, Tromsø, and Bergen were 25.1, 23.3, 23.2, and 21.7% (Figure 4.4).

On method

In this study, correlation analyses are used to illustrate the relationships between key factors. Also, forecasting is used to see a hypothetical development of the market. The sources of secondary data include the Statistics Norway (rent, demographic data, net migration data), Norwegian Central Bank (Key interest rates), and Utleiemegleren (house prices).

Airbnb does not provide historical data, and web-scraping does not provide any historical data either. For historical data, we have used data provided by Airdna. Airdna supplies data on rental types (whole unit, room, and shared room), the unit type (one bedroom, two bedrooms, etc.), historical data from 2008 to 2016, and a cumulative number of rentals including active rentals. Due to changes in the reporting schemes used by Statistics Norway on housing units and Airbnb's time of entry to Norway, we focus on the time span from 2012 to 2016.

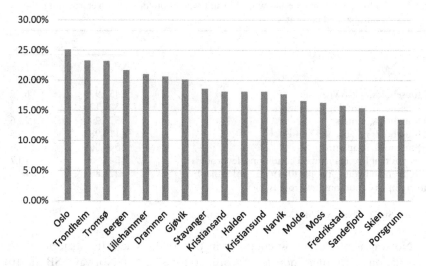

Figure 4.4 Percentage of the people living in rental accommodations.
Source: *Statistics* (2016).

Considering the effect of Airbnb activity on rent levels, we had to rely on data for five major Norwegian cities. For large statistical analysis, this number is small; however, the Statistic Norway only keeps rent data for a few major cities. We acknowledge this as a weakness that could not be overcome.

Analysis

This section focuses on analysis of relationships between Airbnb, house prices, and rental rates.

House prices

Figure 4.5 shows house prices and interest-rate development over the last two decades.

At the national level, house prices show a strong inverse association with the key interest rate ($r = -0{,}672^*$, sig 2-tailed = 0.023). Another factor influencing the house prices at the national level is construction costs (labor + materials, $r = 0{,}788^{**}$, sig 2-tailed = 0,004).

However, to get a better picture, one has to focus on the local level where one can observe a substantial difference in house prices. A correlation study of the effect of Key interest rate on house prices on the regional level showed a strong inverse association between regional housing prices and Key interest rate, except for Stavanger, which as was mentioned previously, was strongly affected by the downturn in oil industry activities (see Table 4.2).

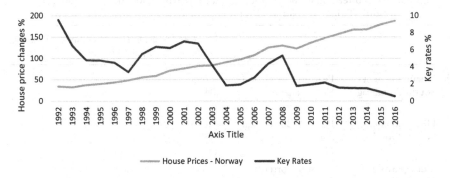

Figure 4.5 House prices and central bank's key rate, 1992–2016.
Sources: Statistics Norway-SSB (2016); Norges Bank (2018).

Table 4.2 Correlation between house prices and central bank interest rate

	Central bank interest rate				Central bank interest rate		
	Pearson Correlation	Sig. (2-tailed)	N		Pearson Correlation	Sig. (2-tailed)	N
Central bank interest rate	1		11	House prices: South-Østlandet	-.678*	,022	11
House prices: country	-.672*	,023	11	House prices: Hedmark and Oppland	-.705*	,015	11
House prices: Oslo with Bærum	-.663*	,026	11	House prices: Agder and Rogaland excluding Stavanger	-.614*	,045	11
House prices: Stavanger	-,557	,075	11	House prices: Vestlandet excluding Bergen	-.707*	,015	11
House prices: Bergen	-.620*	,042	11	House prices: Trøndelag excluding Trondheim	-.698*	,017	11
House prices: Trondheim	-.703*	,016	11	House prices: Northern Norway (Nordland, Troms, Finnmark	-.645*	,032	11
House prices: Akershus excluding Bærum	-.652*	,030	11				

* . Correlation is significant at the 0.05 level (2-tailed).
Correlation: Interest rate – House prices

Checking house prices for effect of *inflation* showed no noticeable association (r = −131, sig 2-tailed = 0,701). However, *unemployment* (a proxy for economic activity, see Table 4.3) showed significant association with house

Table 4.3 The correlation for house prices and unemployment for South-Trondelag, North-Trondelag, Nordland, Troms, and Finmark

		House prices: South-Trondelag, North-Trondelag, Nordland, Troms, and Finmark
Unemployment. South-Trøndelag	Pearson Correlation	−.607[*]
	Sig. (2-tailed)	,048
	N	11
Unemployment. North-Trøndelag	Pearson Correlation	−.643[*]
	Sig. (2-tailed)	,033
	N	11
Unemployment Nordland	Pearson Correlation	−.630[*]
	Sig. (2-tailed)	,038
	N	11
Unemployment Troms	Pearson Correlation	−.756[**]
	Sig. (2-tailed)	,007
	N	11
Unemployment Finnmark	Pearson Correlation	−.731[*]
	Sig. (2-tailed)	,011
	N	11

Source: Statistics Norway-SSB (2016).

prices in *areas in the north of the country* above South Trondelag. Nord Trondelag (r: −0.643, Sig: 0.033), Nordland (r: −0.630, Sig 0.038), Troms (r: −0.756, Sig 0.007), and Finmark (r: − 0.731, Sig 0.011), displayed strong associations between unemployment and house prices. This makes sense, since the three northerly counties: Nordland, Troms, and Finmark, while geographically comprising 34.9% of the country has only 9.3% of its population. A small population (total 480,740) and long distances between towns, make these northern counties, less popular for both industries and internal immigration.

Thus far, it was observed that a significant part of the variance in the house prices could be explained by the Key interest rate, construction costs, and in the Northern regions, unemployment.

The next step was to look at Airbnb and house prices. A correlation analysis of yearly percentage changes in the number of Airbnb units and yearly percentage changes in the house prices in 11 major cities showed very weak statistical power, except in Tromsø. However, based on few observations this test has very weak statistical power and is likely to result in false negative conclusions.

Another way forward was to look at the actual number of units for rents in a given area and based on that try to determine the effect of Airbnb. So, if one takes the total number of apartments, houses (detached-semidetached), etc., and deduct the housing association apartments (where one cannot sublet to others without permission), and those that belong to the city council houses/

apartments (a very small number), one arrives at the total number of apartments or houses that can be rented out. Airbnb has a very small percentage of the total number of potential rental units and therefore cannot affect the house prices in any significant way. According to Statistics Norway, 25% of Oslo's population live in rented accommodation. This does not mean that this population occupies 25% of the rental buildings. If one assumes that some are families and some share, then the actual number will be closer to 15% than 25%; and it is this 15% that we use as our pool of available private rental units (Table 4.4).

Rental rates and Airbnb

As can be seen from Figure 4.6, Airbnb has had considerable growth in Norway in the past five years. The greatest growth has been in the four major cities of Oslo, Bergen, Trondheim, Tromsø, and Stavanger.

Correlation analyses of Airbnb's growth in major cities and rents for 1-, 2-, or 3-bedroom units, don't show any strong correlation, except for Oslo. See Table 4.5 for Airbnb's numbers for Oslo.

Numbers for 2010 and 2011 were simply too small to have any effect and therefore were not included.

In Oslo, one can see that out of 6,075 active rental units in 2016, 76% or 4,623 units were whole units (i.e., studios, apartments, and houses). This makes Airbnb larger than "Fredenborg AS", the largest rental company with 4,000 units, operating in Oslo.

Correlations between Oslo Airbnb and rental prices in Oslo between 2012 and 2016 are shown in Table 4.6.

Table 4.4 Airbnb as a percent of available rental units

Municipality	Nr. of houses* – 2016	15% to rent	Airbnb (whole unit) 2016	Airbnb % of houses* to rent
Oslo	253,889	38,083	4,623	**12.1%**
Bergen	82,055	12,308	1,092	**8.9%**
Stavanger	47,311	7,097	612	**8.6%**
Trondheim	61,359	9,204	375	**4.1%**
Tromsø	32,329	4,849	513	**10.6%**
Kristiansand	33,188	4,978	289	**5.8%**
Fredrikstad	31,150	4,673	67	**1.4%**
Drammen	27,508	4,126	59	**1.4%**
Sandefjord	13,344	2,002	50	**2.5%**
Moss	12,453	1,868	21	**1.1%**
Gjøvik	12,179	1,827	12	**0.7%**
Halden	9,052	1,358	32	**2.4%**

* Detached house + Semi-detached house + Townhouse + Apartments

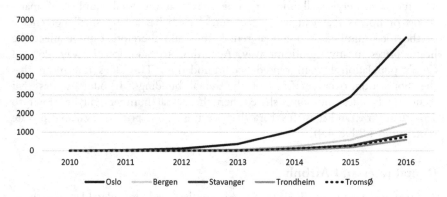

Figure 4.6 Airbnb's growth in Norway.
Source: AirDNA (2018).

Table 4.5 Airbnb rentals in Oslo

	2010	2011	2012	2013	2014	2015	2016
Active Aibnb units (Oslo)	6	29	109	353	1100	2800	6075

Source: Airdna (2018).

Table 4.6 Correlation analysis: Oslo Airbnb and Rents

		Airbnb 1-bedroom	Airbnb 2-bedroom	Airbnb 3-bedroom
Average rent prices 1 bedroom	Pearson Correlation	.959**	.958*	.947*
	Sig. (2-tailed)	,010	,010	,014
	N	5	5	5
Average rent prices 2 bedrooms	Pearson Correlation	.923*	.915*	.900*
	Sig. (2-tailed)	,026	,029	,037
	N	5	5	5
Average rent prices 3 bedrooms	Pearson Correlation	.982**	.971**	.949*
	Sig. (2-tailed)	,003	,006	,014
	N	5	5	5

** . Correlation is significant at the 0.01 level (2-tailed).
* . Correlation is significant at the 0.05 level (2-tailed).

Conclusions

Airbnb has been expanding rapidly in Norway, and in markets, such as Oslo, it has managed to surpass even the largest private rental agencies.

This study has shown that although there is a strong correlation, between the Key interest rate, construction costs, and the house prices, there is no evidence that Airbnb activities, at least until now (in Norway), has had any correlation with prices (except for Oslo).

The data shows that although the rapid expansion of Airbnb in places such as Oslo, Bergen, and Trondheim have slowed, it has increased in other places such as Tromsø, Stavanger, Skien, and Narvik. In addition, although Airbnb's growth in Oslo has slowed down, if it's growth continues unchecked it will soon capture a significant rental market.

To illustrate the significance of this growth in major cities, it is assumed that Airbnb's growth in Oslo, Bergen, Stavanger, Trondheim, and Tromsø will be halved every year from 2017 till 2020 (2017: 50%, 2018: 25%, 2019: 12,5%, and 2020: 6.5). The resulting estimation of Airbnb growth is shown in Table 4.7.

As can be seen, even with a 50% reduction in growth year-on-year, one is still talking about significant numbers, especially when one considers the actual increase in new houses that are being built. According to Boligprodusentenes Forening-House producers Association (Homebuilders association, 2016), only 4,000 new buildings were started in 2017, against the actual need of over 6,500 per year. The 4,000 unit represents 1.5% growth. These numbers vary significantly across the cities, suggesting that in some places the effect of Airbnb may be especially significant.

To be safe, it is assumed that housing construction will take-off, and instead of 1.5% per year, it is increased to 10% per year, over the next three years in all major cities. So while construction of new buildings is increased by 10% per year Airbnb's expansion is halved year-on-year until 2020. As can be seen from Table 4.8, in 2020, Airbnb still has occupied close to 25% of all available rental units in Oslo (1-, 2-, 3-room, apartments, and houses); and the situation is no better for Tromsø, Bergen, or Stavanger either. These are significant numbers.

This study concludes that although at present, Airbnb and its clones do not represent a major problem, if they are allowed to expand unhindered, they

Table 4.7 Airbnb's projected growth based on the assumption of the year-on-year halving of growth

		Percent growth per year		
	Airbnb *2016*	*50%* *2017*	*25%* *2018*	*12.5%* *2019*	*6.125%* *2020*
Oslo	4,623	6,935	8,668	9,752	10,385
Bergen	1,092	1,638	2,048	2,303	2,453
Stavanger	612	918	1,148	1,291	1,375
Trondheim	375	563	703	791	842
Tromsø	513	770	962	1,082	1,152

Table 4.8 Estimated growth in available housing and Airbnb rentals in selected cities

Municipality	No. of residential buildings*, 2016	10% increase in no. of residential buildings*, 2020	15% of residential buildings to let	Airbnb (whole units), 2016	Airbnb as % of available rental residential buildings
Oslo	253,889	279277,9	41,892	10,385	**24.8%**
Bergen	82,055	90260,5	13,539	2,453	**18.1%**
Stavanger	47,311	52042,1	7,806	1,375	**17.6%**
Trondheim	61,359	67494,9	10,124	842	**8.3%**
Tromsø	32,329	35561,9	5,334	1,152	**21.6%**

* Detached house + Semi-detached house + Townhouse + Apartments

can cause a house/apartment rental shortage for the people in need of rental dwellings in respective municipalities.

To address this problem authorities can force hosts (a) to register all Airbnb rentals with the municipalities especially for the whole units; and/or (b) levy a hotel tax, and/or (c) apply a one-week minimum stay for the guests (Japanese solution). Safety inspections are another thing that could be considered. Room sharing and single rooms in lived-in dwelling may be exempt from these conditions, since they not only represent a minor share of the total, but also are used to supplement the family income.

This study has presented some cases to stimulate further research into relationships between sharing economy and real estate and rental markets. The relationships between factors discussed in this paper may be further tested through quantitative research preferably based on longitudinal datasets.

References

AirDNA. Data & Analytics for Vacation Rental Hosts and Airbnb Investors. (2018). Retrieved August 20, 2018, from www.airdna.co/.

Barron, K., Kung, E., & Proserpio, D. (2017). *The Sharing Economy and Housing Affordability: Evidence from Airbnb.* New York: ACM.

Barron, K., Kung, E., & Proserpio, D. (2018). *The Sharing Economy and Housing Affordability: Evidence from Airbnb* (SSRN Scholarly Paper No. ID 3006832). Rochester, NY: Social Science Research Network. Retrieved from https://papers.ssrn.com/abstract=3006832.

Belsky, E., & Prakken, J. (2004). Housing Wealth Effects: Housing's Impact on Wealth Accumulation. *Wealth Distribution, and Consumer Spending,'a Paper Prepared for the National Association of Realtors National Center for Real Estate Research.*

Beltratti, A., & Morana, C. (2010). International House Prices and Macroeconomic Fluctuations. *Journal of Banking & Finance, 34*(3), 533–545.

Boforhold, registerbasert, 2015. (2016). Statistisk Sentralbyrå. Retrieved from www.ssb.no/bygg-bolig-og-eiendom/statistikker/boforhold/aar/2016-09-29.

Boone, A. (2018, March 5). What Airbnb Did to New York City. Retrieved August 15, 2018, from www.citylab.com/equity/2018/03/what-airbnb-did-to-new-york-city/552749/.

Botsman, R., & Rogers, R. (2010). *What's Mine Is Yours*. *London: Collins*. Retrieved from https://tantor-marketing-assets.s3.amazonaws.com/sellsheets/1920_MineIsYours.pdf.

Capozza, D.R., Hendershott, P.H., Mack, C., & Mayer, C.J. (2002). *Determinants of Real House Price Dynamics*. Cambridge, MA: National Bureau of Economic Research.

Carter, G. (2015). *Secrets of the Sharing Economy: Unofficial Guide to Using Airbnb, Uber, & More to Earn $1000's* (Kindle).

France-Presse, A. (2016, May 1). Berlin's Government Legislates against Airbnb. *The Guardian*. Retrieved from www.theguardian.com/technology/2016/may/01/berlin-authorities-taking-stand-against-airbnb-rental-boom.

Gallin, J. (2008). The Long-Run Relationship between House Prices and Rents. *Real Estate Economics, 36*(4), 635–658. https://doi.org/10.1111/j.1540-6229.2008.00225.x.

Girouard, N., Kennedy, M., Van Den Noord, P., & André, C. (2006). *Recent House Price Developments*. Paris: OECD Publishing.

Himmelberg, C., Mayer, C., & Sinai, T. (2005). Assessing High House Prices: Bubbles, Fundamentals and Misperceptions. *The Journal of Economic Perspectives, 19*(4), 67–92.

Jacobsen, D.H., & Naug, B.E. (2005). What Drives House Prices? *Norges Bank. Economic Bulletin; Oslo, 76*(1), 29–41.

Kartlegging av delingsøkonomien i Norge. (2016, April 5). Kommunal- Og Moderniserings-departementet (KMD) Ved Avdeling for IKT Og Fornying. Retrieved from https://kgv.doffin.no/ctm/Supplier/Documents/Folder/143896.

Norges Bank. (2018). Monetary Policy. Retrieved August 20, 2018, from www.norges-bank.no/en/Monetary-policy/.

Prisindeks for brukte boliger. Statistikkbanken. (2018). Retrieved August 20, 2018, from www.ssb.no/statbank/list/bpi.

Quattrone, G., Proserpio, D., Quercia, D., Capra, L., & Musolesi, M. (2016). Who Benefits from the "sharing" Economy of Airbnb? In *Proceedings of the 25th International Conference on World Wide Web* (pp. 1385–1394). Republic and Canton of Geneva, Switzerland: International World Wide Web Conferences Steering Committee. https://doi.org/10.1145/2872427.2874815

Rosenberg, Z. (2018, January 30). Airbnb Leads to Median Rent Increase, Promotes Gentri-fication: Study. Retrieved August 15, 2018, from https://ny.curbed.com/2018/1/30/16950424/airbnb-gentrification-nyc-median-rent-study.

Segú, M. (2018). *Do Short-term Rent Platforms Affect Rents? Evidence from Airbnb in Barcelona*. Barcelona: IEB.

Sheppard, S., & Udell, A. (2016). *Do Airbnb Properties Affect House Prices?* (Department of Economics Working Papers No. 2016–03). Department of Economics, Williams College. Retrieved from https://ideas.repec.org/p/wil/wileco/2016-03.html.

Statista. (2016). Homeownership Rate in Europe by Country 2016 | Statistic. Retrieved March 23, 2018, from www.statista.com/statistics/246355/home-ownership-rate-in-europe/.

Statistics Norway-SSB. (2016). 4,2 Millioner Bor I Eid Bolig. Retrieved December 19, 2016, from www.ssb.no/bygg-bolig-og-eiendom/statistikker/boforhold/aar/2016-09-29.

Svalbardposten, A. (2017, September 15). Uten Kontroll. Retrieved March 23, 2018, from http://svalbardposten.no/index.php?page=vis_nyhet&NyhetID=8868.

Svalbardposten, A. (2018, February 8). Fortviler over Boligmarkedet. Retrieved March 23, 2018, from http://svalbardposten.no/index.php?page=vis_nyhet&NyhetID=9384.

Tsatsaronis, K., & Zhu, H. (2004). What Drives Housing Price Dynamics: Cross-country Evidence.

Wachsmuth, D., & Weisler, A. (2017). Airbnb and the Rent Gap: Gentrification through the Sharing Economy. *Environment and Planning A: Economy and Space.* 0308518X18778038.

Wakatsuki, W., & Ripley, Y. (2016, February 23). Airbnb Faces Headaches in Booming Japanese Market. Retrieved February 24, 2016, from http://money.cnn.com/2016/02/23/news/companies/airbnb-japan-challenges/index.html.

Wig, K. (2016, June 29). Nye Beregninger Viser Enda Sterkere Rift Om Oslo-boliger. Retrieved March 15, 2017, from http://e24.no/article/23726304.

Woolf, N. (2016, December 3). Airbnb Regulation Deal with London and Amsterdam Marks Dramatic Policy Shift. *The Guardian.* Retrieved from www.theguardian.com/technology/2016/dec/03/airbnb-regulation-london-amsterdam-housing.

5 Digital entrepreneurs in the sharing economy

A case study on Airbnb and regional economic development in Norway

Birgit Leick, Mehtap Aldogan Eklund and Bjørnar Karlsen Kivedal

Introduction

In the present book chapter, we focus on technological innovation through digitisation that takes place in the sharing economy and review the link between such digital entrepreneurship and regional economic development. Although the stream of research on entrepreneurship and its impact on regional economic growth and development is abundant (Acs & Armington, 2004; Carree & Thurik, 2003), there is still a gap in the literature about the sharing economy with both its opportunities and necessities for digital entrepreneurship and its effect on regional economic development. Airbnb is one of the big players in the global sharing economy and has a huge impact on traditional accommodation services. Although the business model of the company is problematised as a disruptive innovation that challenges traditional accommodation (Zervas et al., 2017), it is rarely considered as an entrepreneurial activity in itself, which is driven by individuals that offer an innovative way of accommodation to the tourist market. This book chapter addresses this gap and defines digital entrepreneurs in the sharing economy as the suppliers of short-term housing to the Airbnb-brokered accommodation market. More specifically, our main objective is to provide the first contribution to this emerging topic with an empirical analysis that links the development of Airbnb rentals with the selected regional economic development indicator. We use data on Airbnb rentals for the Norwegian region of Østfold to map the potential connection of these entrepreneurs in the sharing economy with unemployment in the region.

The message of the chapter is therefore threefold: First, Airbnb represents a distinct type of digital entrepreneurship that challenges the traditional understanding of entrepreneurs. Second, digital entrepreneurship in the sharing economy does not only change markets and technologies, but it also affects regional economic development. Finally, there is some first empirical evidence that Airbnb-based entrepreneurs may be motivated by an extra market demand that is anticipated for accommodation in the region (opportunity entrepreneurship) rather than the need for generating income due to a lack of regional job opportunities (necessity entrepreneurship).

The remainder of the book chapter is structured as follows. First, the theoretical background and literature review provide the readers with the definitions and the theoretical framework for the conceptual links between the sharing economy, digital entrepreneurship, and regional economic growth and development. Second, the Airbnb case is briefly introduced, and its effect on the county of Østfold, a secondary touristic destination in Norway, is illustrated, based on selected regional economic development indicators. Finally, the conclusion provides a summary of the key arguments and an outlook on future research.

Economic theories and entrepreneurship: an overview

Traditional economic growth theories explain land, labor, and capital as the primary factors of production (Baumol, 2010). For instance, neo-classical growth theory focuses merely on the contribution of labour and capital to economic development and growth, and, as the mathematics of equilibrium theory, it does not leave room for new ideas, innovation, and initiative-taking in terms of entrepreneurial actions (Wennekers & Thurik, 1999). Generally speaking, entrepreneurship and technology did not fit in traditional economic theories. However, modern economics has shown that economic growth cannot fully be explained by the production factors land, labor, and capital alone; therefore, entrepreneurship is meanwhile recognised as the fourth factor of production and vital component in the process of economic growth. The shift from a managed to the entrepreneurial economy has strengthened the significance of small and digital entrepreneurs (Baumol, 1968), which also fits entrepreneurship in the digital age (Prieger et al., 2016).

In this book chapter, we follow a *Schumpeterian view of entrepreneurship* by acknowledging digital technologies as an innovation (Oner & Kunday, 2016) that is oriented towards process technology innovation and technological innovation (North & Smallbone, 2000). In line with Richter et al. (2015), we argue that entrepreneurship in the digital age incorporates new business opportunities, which lead to a "*Schumpeterian* creative destruction" by enabling new goods and services that are, for example, in the sharing economy, shared among customers and users and facilitated by technological development such as digitalisation (Geissinger et al., 2018). The *Schumpeterian* approach also posits that innovation and entrepreneurship facilitate economic growth (Angulo-Guerrero et al., 2017) by predicting that "an increase in the number of entrepreneurs leads to an increase in economic growth" (Urbano & Aparicio, 2016, p. 35). With regard to digitalisation, Sussan and Acs (2017, p. 56) emphasise that "the digital entrepreneurial ecosystem is composed of *Schumpeterian (1911) entrepreneurs* creating digital companies and innovative goods and services for many users and agents in the global economy" (see Schumpeter, 1911).

In addition to the economics literature, management research views innovation as a direct manifestation of entrepreneurship, which represents the intermediate process linking entrepreneurship to economic growth (Wennekers &

Thurik, 1999). It has also been proposed that in the modern entrepreneurial economy, information, communication, and technology (ICT) revolutions, along with globalisation and the digitalised environment, are the driving aspects of both the sharing economy and economic growth (Richter et al., 2017).

Literature review

This section introduces both relevant definitions and the conceptual understanding of digital entrepreneurship in connection with the sharing economy. By establishing a link between the two streams in the literature, the sharing economy is described as a specific form of digital entrepreneurship (see Figure 5.1).

Entrepreneurship in the traditional versus the digitised world

The typical entrepreneur is described as a risk-taking, independent and growth- or profit-oriented individual who is seeking, identifying and using opportunities in markets (Carland et al., 1984). Moreover, the process of starting a business is usually associated with elements such as the recognition of existing entrepreneurial opportunities, the development of a marketable product, and the creation of new value (Shane & Venkataraman, 2000). These elements are also valid for entrepreneurial ventures in the digital age (Hull et al., 2007; Standing & Mattsson, 2018). However, entrepreneurship in the digital age differs substantially from the entrepreneurship of the non-digitised

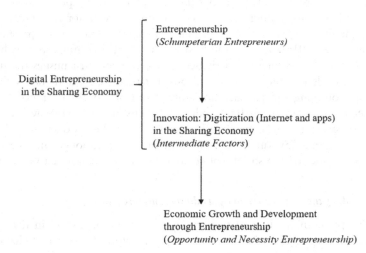

Figure 5.1 Theoretical framework on the link between digital entrepreneurship and economic growth and development.

world (Standing & Mattsson, 2018) for several reasons. Digital technology as an enabler of digital entrepreneurship magnifies the opportunities for individuals who want to become entrepreneurs because there is an enormous growth of such technologies and technology-based opportunities; moreover, the usage of digital technologies lowers the costs of setting up a business virtually (Hull et al., 2007). For instance, Grimes (2003) shows that access to high-speed internet is an important factor for benefiting from the digital economy, especially in rural areas.

In the literature, it is acknowledged that there is a need to conceptualise what digital entrepreneurship represents and what it is constituted of (Giones & Brem, 2017; Richter et al., 2017; Sussan & Acs, 2017). Open questions refer, for example, to the theoretical foundations of the business models associated with digital entrepreneurship (Richter et al., 2017; Standing & Mattsson, 2018), the distinction between digital technology entrepreneurship and other digital entrepreneurial activities (Giones & Brem, 2017), and a systems perspective on digital entrepreneurial ecosystems (Sussan & Acs, 2017).

The emerging strand of literature gives some answers to these open questions, which might help to understand better the characteristics of digital entrepreneurship. For example, there is a change in the role of consumers as well as producers. In a traditional business world, producers are new business-start-ups that sell a new, innovative good or service to individuals or other companies buying it, whereas these roles are much more blurry for digital entrepreneurship. Producers of digital content do not necessarily have to be self-employed persons, but they can be virtually anyone, including the users themselves (Haefliger et al., 2010; Sussan & Acs, 2017). In a similar vein, the users of digital content are not just receiving a product for usage, but they might also give input regarding new variants and versions or improved types of the product sold, for example, regarding design, functionality, and practicability, thereby turning into "prosumers" (Weitzenboeck, 2015). In fact, often, there is a "tribal community" of highly innovative users with intensive activities on social media that pushes the digital product towards reaching a large, and broad, target group, and their effect in terms of promoting the product (including word-of-mouth) is crucial for the producer (Kozinets et al., 2010; Standing & Mattsson, 2018). Finally, the open digital infrastructure alters the spatial organisation of the production and consumption processes (Sussan & Acs, 2017) because it is no longer necessary that producers are located at a specific place, and users come to a place to consume.

Understanding the sharing economy as digital entrepreneurship

The multiple combinations of technology and entrepreneurship in the digital age have an important socio-economic impact. Before defining and characterising the essence of digital entrepreneurship, we distinguish it from digital technology entrepreneurship (Giones & Brem, 2017) in the following way: In *digital technology entrepreneurship*, new goods and services brought to the market are based on ICT technologies only, and entrepreneurial activities are related to the generation of ICT-based smart devices with the help of the internet, for example, smartphones. By contrast, *digital entrepreneurship* refers to new goods and services, which are based on the internet, e.g., apps and where technology is one input factor among others. Hereby, the innovative product or service is typically running in a cloud and uses big data or artificial intelligence (Giones & Brem, 2017). Airbnb, Snapchat, and Uber are common examples.

Following this distinction, we refer to the broad definition of digital entrepreneurship given by Sussan and Acs (2017, p. 66), who define such entrepreneurs as "any agent that is engaged in any venture be it commercial, social, government, or corporate that uses digital technologies". Since we argue that the entrepreneurial process with digital entrepreneurship is determined by the same generic elements that apply for "traditional" entrepreneurship (Hull et al., 2007; Kraus et al., 2019; Standing & Mattsson, 2018), the various entrepreneurial activities, which are based on collaborative consumption, and the use of digital technologies in the sharing economy, form part of this understanding of digital entrepreneurship (Giones & Brem, 2017). This is echoed by Richter et al. (2017, p. 301) who identify the following opportunities associated with the sharing economy: the occupation of niches in markets; the innovativeness of an entrepreneurial idea; the finding of a yet unknown path; rule-breaking; and the discard of an existing business model in favour of a new model being established. All these elements can be linked back to various entrepreneurial activities taking place in the sharing economy.

Taken together, we claim that the sharing economy represents a distinct type of digital entrepreneurship based on the internet, and makes use of digital technologies (e.g., cloud-based services, a peer-to-peer platform) to offer either physical or intangible, digital goods and services (Cheng, 2016; Giones & Brem, 2017). For example, the taxi driver service Uber in the sharing economy delivers a physical product, but a large part of the service provision is digitally organised (Sussan & Acs, 2017). This is also the case for Airbnb, which uses a digital process to connect the consumers of accommodation with its suppliers, but eventually provides non-digital accommodation services.

Understanding the sharing economy as regional entrepreneurship

The connection between the sharing economy and regional entrepreneurship is rarely made in the academic literature. One obvious explanation is the dominance of large, global ventures such as Airbnb and Uber, which have quickly grown out of their business start-up period and turned into global players. Therefore, at first glance, it can be argued that international entrepreneurship and business theories might apply better to such global cases. However, a common characteristic of these business ventures in the sharing economy is that a small, and mostly regional, initiative was at their origin, which subsequently underwent a process of rapid company growth, nearly from the earliest days of their inception. In fact, Richter et al. (2015) high-light that sharing economy start-ups are influenced by huge business oppor-tunities with enormous growth prospects, but at the same time, they face fierce competition. Moreover, the business model of Airbnb can be character-ised by the presence of a global corporation that is connected with numerous regional entrepreneurs: these are private persons renting out available housing space via Airbnb, and thus they behave entrepreneurially by offering an innovative service on a market that meets a certain demand. Altogether, the variety of opportunities in the sharing economy is vast, and they are repre-sented on the regional level. Gössling and Michael Hall (2019, p. 78) state: "Platforms can be local, crowdfunded initiatives, global corporations backed by venture capital, or government initiatives. The latter can also be a public service, that is travel information or a profit-oriented state-owned enterprise".

   Still, the empirical evidence of regional entrepreneurship in the sharing economy is scarce. The available case studies show that tourism is an industry that offers such opportunities. Grèzes et al. (2016) illustrate how crowdsour-cing technologies were used in a Swiss tourism cluster to develop new ideas and attract new business opportunities for the regional tourism industry. Gyi-móthy and Meged (2018) report about a Danish municipality that established a sharing-economy based communitarian tourism initiative to make the des-tination more attractive to visitors. The core of the initiative is a walking trail. Both case studies highlight how social and government entrepreneurship is enabled by the sharing economy and that it can be anchored in a region (Mosedale & Voll, 2017). Liu (2014) also states that the sharing economy can be a relevant industry for tourism events, such as the European Capitals of Culture events. Such entrepreneurial opportunities also exist outside tourism, for example, with urban fashion libraries (Pedersen & Netter, 2015). Taken together, regional entrepreneurship in the sharing economy can be found in various sectors with roots in a given region, such as retail trade, tourism, food economies, farming, and cultural and creative industries, but tourism is the most prominent regional industry benefitting from sharing-economy entrepreneurs.

Entrepreneurship, digital entrepreneurship, and regional economic growth and development

In the following, we give an overview of the functions that entrepreneurs including digital entrepreneurs have with regard to regional economic devel-opment, such as job creation and investments, the usage of unused resources, and the provision of social capital in terms of building and strengthening social communities. On top of the well-known stylised facts, we explore how digital entrepreneurship can affect regional economic development. Generally, we follow the definition by Stimson et al. (2006, p. 6), which characterises regional economic development as follows:

Regional economic development is the application of economic processes and resources available to a region that results in the sustainable development of, and desired economic outcomes for a region and that meet the values and expectations of business, of residents and visitors.

In the literature, many empirical studies have measured the contribution of entrepreneurship to economic growth in developing, developed, and OECD countries. Acs et al. (2012), Braunerhjelm et al. (2010), and Mueller (2007) reported a positive relationship between entrepreneurship and productivity. This is consistent with Valliere and Peterson (2009), Sautet (2013), and Van Stel et al. (2005), who all found a positive association between entrepreneurship and economic growth in developed and OECD countries, but a negative link in low-income countries (Prieger et al., 2016). Other studies, such as Van Stel et al. (2010) and Prieger et al. (2016), however, did not find a significant relationship between entrepreneurship and economic development in rich countries. With regard to the regional level, it is highlighted that entrepreneurship is a regional phenomenon (Sternberg, 2011) and plays a key role in regional economic development (Malecki, 1993). Acs and Armington (2004) show that regional employment growth is caused by factors such as entrepreneurial activity, agglomeration effects, and human capital. Hence, regional economic growth can be caused by increased entrepreneurship, which leads to reduced unemployment.

For the sharing economy, however, Joshi and Yermish (2000), Sussan and Acs (2017), and Richter et al. (2017) all mention that research on this direction of entrepreneurship is still in its infancy. As a result, there is a little knowledge available about what role the entrepreneur plays in the development of the sharing economy and which potential such an entrepreneur can have in terms of the impact on regional economic growth and development. Most of the arguments brought forward are of theoretical nature. Haefliger et al. (2010) state that, in modern digital entrepreneurial ecosystems, the writing of a business app by means of the usage of digital tools is one of the most common types of digital entrepreneurship. When it comes to the potential impact of such entrepreneurial activities, Acs (2006, p. 97) posits this as follows: "Entrepreneurs create new businesses, and new businesses, in turn, create jobs, intensify competition, and may even increase productivity through technological change. High measured levels of entrepreneurship will thus translate directly into high levels of economic growth".

However, in reality, this link is more complex. A common typology of entrepreneurship in a region is "opportunity" versus "necessity entrepreneurship"; "opportunity entrepreneurship" implies business start-ups because of the available business opportunities on the market (for example, within a given region), whereas "necessity entrepreneurship" is related to business start-ups emerging due to a lack of available traditional jobs in the region (Acs, 2006). Depending on the specific case, entrepreneurship in the sharing economy can take both forms. On the one hand, Airbnb rentals can be driven by opportunities because already available unused resources, e.g., vacant houses, apartments or rooms, may be utilised as an opportunity to turn into an entrepreneur. This would apply for a high demand for tourist accommodation in a given region that would leave room for additional providers outside the traditional accommodation sector. On the other hand, Airbnb rentals can also be driven by necessities rather than opportunities, i.e., the renting out of available housing space would primarily be meant to generate extra income, for example, in a region with high unemployment levels (Giacomin et al., 2011). Both motivations for digital entrepreneurship may imply regional economic growth because they may affect the regional demand for tourist services and involve a higher level of entrepreneurial activities in a region. Because of this, entrepreneurship as in the case of Airbnb may have self-reinforcing effects on regional economic development.

Airbnb as a case of digital entrepreneurs in Østfold, Norway

The sharing economy has been particularly shaped by the two big players Airbnb and Uber, but the variety of business start-ups in this field is much wider. For example, the initially French travel hosting service "Nightswapping" was founded in 2012, just a few years after Airbnb started its activities, and the company has recently been merged with the large HomeExchange group network, which incorporates several sharing economy providers in the field of accommodation, travel and leisure services (HomeExchange, 2019). In Germany, the initiative "Foodsharing" (Foodsharing, 2019) started out as a collaborative consumption initiative in 2011, aiming to avoid waste of edible food by supermarket/grocery chains and users who could register and share food through various platforms. These examples show that there are various entrepreneurial opportunities linked to digital entrepreneurship.

Airbnb: company background

In the sharing economy, the company Airbnb belongs to the up-end industries on a global scale and ranks among the most representative cases for the new breed of global companies using digital technology, digital entrepreneurship, and innovation (Cheng, 2016; Sussan & Acs, 2017). Airbnb, Inc. (formerly known as AirBed & Breakfast, Inc) was founded by three pioneers of digital entrepreneurship in San Francisco, California, back in 2008, and it has offices across North America, Europe, and Asia. It operates in hospitality and tourism services without owning any real estates. The company offers a global online marketplace, and its services are accessible through its website and mobile applications. It works as a brokerage firm and gets a commission for every booking with a provider registered with Airbnb (Bloomberg., 2018). Large-scale, privately owned, and venture-capital funded enterprises such as Airbnb provide employment globally, but most notably connect the web of small digital entrepreneurs – which can be both professional business people and private persons owning real estate – with a global market by means of internet platforms and mobile Apps (Cheng & Foley, 2018).

Airbnb and economic development in Østfold: descriptive statistics

In this case study, we aim to look into the growth in the number of Airbnb listings in Østfold (provided by data from Airdna), compare it to the two neighbouring regions of Akershus and Oslo, and we relate Airbnb's growth to selected economic factors, which we consider to represent regional economic development indicators, both regarding the regional business cycle and tourism.

Østfold is one of 18 counties in Norway and is located in the southeast of the country, bordering Sweden. After the industrial revolution, the Norwegian economy has been largely based on the gas/oil and fishery sectors (Ministry of Trade, Industry, and Fisheries, 2019). In the past, these sectors as well as wood, chemical, and mineral industries have been dominant for the regional economy in Østfold, and today, selected industries such as construction, food and machineries are dominant (Selstad, 2003). Altogether, the region is considered as a traditionally rural-peripheral area with an agricultural background and a prevalence of less dynamic industries, compared to Norway as a whole (Selstad, 2003).

Therefore, it is obvious that Østfold itself is not the most prominent, typical, and internationally recognised touristic region in Norway, but despite this, it contains some of the "most visited" and historically significant sites in Norway, such as the fortresses in Fredrikstad and Halden. The summer seasons are important for tourism in Østfold. However, tourism itself as a regional industry does not play a large role in the county's regional economic development (OECD, 2018). Due to this, Østfold is considered as a secondary tourist destination in Norway, which might offer additional opportunities for Airbnb-based digital entrepreneurs; they can create additional demand for accommodation in a regional market that hosts mainly traditional accommodation providers, such as hotels, bed-and-breakfast pensions, rented cabins, camping sites, etc. In addition to the tourism aspect, we have selected Østfold because of the county's high unemployment rate compared to the country average. Especially after 2009, it is one of the highest in Norway (OECD, 2018) at an average rate of 3.1% from 2009 to 2018 compared to the national average of 2.5% for the same period based on unemployment rates in November each year (see also Figure 5.4). The unemployment rate, also, is a variable that we investigate in our model in this book chapter.

Indeed, with regard to the number of available units from 2015 until present,[1] Airbnb has grown substantially in Østfold from one listing only in the end of 2015 to 798 listings in April 2019 (Figure 5.2), both in the largest cities (Fredrikstad, Sarpsborg, Moss and Halden) and in rural municipalities. The number of listings in Østfold also doubled from the end of 2016 until the present. By contrast, Airbnb's growth seems to be only moderate, for

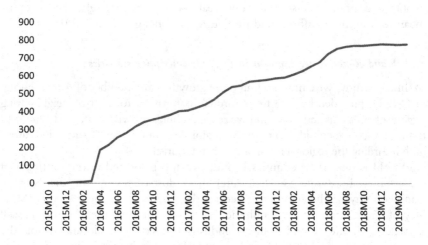

Figure 5.2 Number of Airbnb listings in Østfold, monthly data (October 2015–March 2019). Source: Airdna (2019) and authors' calculations.

example in the capital city of Oslo,[2] which is only about a 110 km distance from Østfold and that hosts a larger tourist industry.

If we assume that Airbnb works as an alternative to traditional accommodation options, the growth of Airbnb rentals should be compared with the development of total overnight stays in Østfold over the past few years. Figure 5.3 shows that there is a high degree of seasonality in the number of overnight stays both in Østfold and in a total of Norway, while the neighbouring counties of Akershus and Oslo seem to be less affected by seasonality. Furthermore, we see an increase in the trend for all three counties and Norway in general from 2005 until 2015, but after 2015, it seems like the growth has flattened in Oslo as well as in Norway overall, while it is still positive in Akershus, and it turns negative for Østfold when we look at the peak month of July. This decline may be a result of an increase in Airbnb listings that might substitute traditional accommodation for tourists, or it may be a result of the overall declining demand for accommodation in Østfold. Compared to the neighbouring counties, however, Østfold does not experience an increase in the number of tourists received over the past years. Altogether, as the descriptive data suggest, the strong increase in Airbnb listings in Østfold in the past few years coincides with a moderate decline in traditional overnight stays starting in the peak months of 2016 until the present.

With regard to regional economic development indicators, Østfold performs lower than the rest of Norway (OECD, 2018). For example, the per-capita GDP in 2014 (USD 32,323) was lower than in Akershus (USD 43,702) or the OECD average (USD 39,828). The labour market in Østfold has a focus on the manufacturing sector (OECD, 2018), notably around

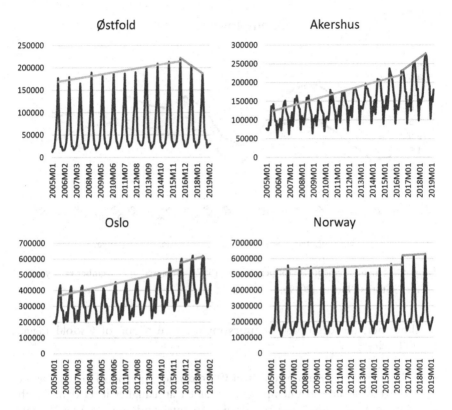

Figure 5.3 Number if overnight stays in Østfold, Akershus, Oslo and Norway in total, January 2005–March 2019.

Note: This variable measures one person accommodated one night at a collective accommodation establishment such as hotels, camping sites, etc. Linear trendlines for the peak months July 2005–2016 (dotted) and for July 2016–2018 (grey).

Source: Statistics Norway (2019a).

Halden, Fredrikstad, and Sarpsborg. By contrast, rural regions in Østfold are dominated by forestry and agriculture. One of the available indicators at the county-level for regional economic development in Østfold is the unemployment rate, shown in Figure 5.4. While the unemployment rate in Østfold seemed to follow the country trend from 1999 until the financial crisis in 2008/2009, it stabilised at a higher level than the country average after this period. With regard to regional employment opportunities, the cities of Fredrikstad-Sarpsborg provided 7% and Halden 1% of all jobs within the grand region of Oslo, Akershus, and Østfold, while 92% of all new jobs were located in Oslo and Akershus (OECD, 2018); similarly, employment in the recent past increased at a much lower rate in Østfold than in these two neighbouring regions of Norway.

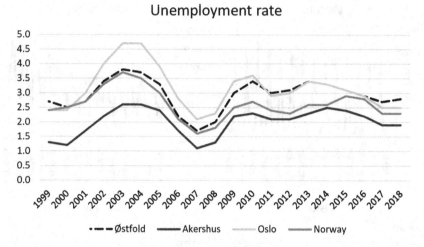

Figure 5.4 Unemployment rate for persons age 15–74, measured in November each year. Source: Statistics Norway (2019b).

Altogether, the descriptive statistics for the case region of Østfold suggest the following:

- The increase in Airbnb rentals in Østfold since the end of 2015, together with the decline in unemployment (albeit at a higher level than for the rest of the country) and the decline in total traditional overnight stays, shows that there may be different factors that can explain these trends. Airbnb's growth in terms of rentals in Østfold might be driven by a "hotelization" of the regional accommodation industry (see Lee, 2016), leaving room for alternative accommodation modes of tourists. In this case, entrepreneurs offering Airbnb rentals can be motivated by either necessities, opportunities, or both.
- The growth of Airbnb rentals may, however, also be linked to small, and limited, regional labour markets that offer little alternatives and push individuals with available housing space to offer such rentals and generate extra income from this source. In this case, the entrepreneurial person would be motivated by necessities rather than opportunities.

ARDL model

In the following, we use data for the number of Airbnb units, the number of traditional overnight stays, and the unemployment rate for Østfold to compute a regression analysis with an autoregressive distributed-lagged (ARDL) model.

The sample runs from October 2015 to March 2019 and provides three variables: one for Airbnb rentals, one for traditional overnight stays (such as hotels, camping cabins, etc.) and the unemployment rate (which seeks to explain the macroeconomic development on the regional level). We attempt to establish a link between those three markets with this limited data set. Tests for stationarity using the augmented Dickey-Fuller test (including a trend, a constant, and seasonal effects) cannot reject the null hypothesis of non-stationarity (i.e., a unit root) in any of the variables. If we find co-integration, we can test for long-run Granger causality using the ARDL model (see, for example, Pesaran & Shin, 1998; Pesaran et al., 2001). Hence, the ARDL model is a suitable model to estimate the relationship between these variables since they are non-stationary and there is the possibility of cointegration that we would like to test, in addition to testing for Granger causality.

We follow among others Narayan and Smyth (2005) and use the ARDL model to test for the direction of causality in the long run. This is done by estimating the ARDL model and testing for co-integration using the bounds test (see Pesaran et al., 2001), and finally to investigate Granger causality through the estimated error correction effects given that co-integration is present.

The ARDL model that we use will then be expressed as:

$$Y_t = a_0 + a_1 t + \sum_{i=1}^{p} \psi_i Y_{t-i} + \sum_{j=0}^{q_1} \beta_{1j} X_{1,t-j} + \sum_{j=0}^{q_2} \beta_{2j} X_{2,t-j} + \varepsilon_t \tag{1}$$

where the Y_t, $X_{1,t}$ and $X_{2,t}$ are the number of Airbnb listings, the unemployment rate and the number of "traditional" overnight stays in month t for Østfold.[3] The model is estimated three times, using each of the three variables as a dependent variable in order to investigate the direction of causality. Furthermore, p is the number of lags for the dependent variable, while q_1 and q_2 are the number of lags for the two independent variables, such that the number of lags may be different for the two explanatory variables. In addition, we include seasonal dummies (not shown in (1)) as exogenous variables, a restricted trend, and a constant, and ε_t is an error term. This provides an ARDL(p, q_1, q_2)-model. The number of lags is determined by Schwarz information criteria. The lags of the dependent variable will then be the autoregressive part and the explanatory variables (with their lags) will be the distributed part of the ARDL model.

Given that each model is well specified and we see signs of co-integration between the variables (investigated through the bounds test), the sign and significance of the error correction term, and the coefficients in the levels equation, we can determine whether we have Granger causality. Furthermore, (1) may be reformulated as an error correction model as:

$$\Delta Y_t = \sum_{i=1}^{5} \gamma_0 Y_{t-i} + \sum_{i=0}^{5} \gamma_{1,i} X_{1,t-i} + \sum_{i=0}^{4} \gamma_{2,i} X_{2,t-i} + \sum_{j=1}^{11} \theta_j S_j + const$$
$$+ \Pi coint_{t-1} + \varepsilon_t$$

where $coint_{t-1}$ contains the cointegration vector, which describes the long run relationship between the variables, and $const$ is a constant term, Δ is the first difference operator, i.e., $\Delta Y_t = Y_t - Y_{t-1}$ and S are the seasonal dummies. If $-1 < \gamma_3 < 0$ and it is significant, we have indications of long-run causality from the explanatory variables $X_{1,t}$ and $X_{2,t}$ to the dependent variable Y_t. Table 5.1 shows the F-statistics for the bounds test, including the error correction term, the coefficients in the levels equation (where β_j is the coefficient on variable X_j (for $j = 1, 2$) and β_{trend} is the coefficient on the trend), as well as the F-statistics for the Lagrange multiplier test for autocorrelation in the residuals with two lags (LM(2)), and its p-value for the null hypothesis of no serial correlation and the F-statitic and the p-value for the Breusch-Pagan-Godfrey test for the null hypothesis of no heteroskedasticity (HETTEST). The numbers in parentheses below the estimated coefficients are standard errors and asterisks imply significance at the 1% (***), 5% (**) and 10% (*) significance level. In

Table 5.1 Results from ARDL estimations

	MODEL 1	MODEL 2	MODEL 3
Y_t	Airbnb$_t$	overnight$_t$	unemp$_t$
$X_{1,t}$	overnight$_t$	Airbnb$_t$	overnight$_t$
$X_{2,t}$	unemp$_t$	unemp$_t$	Airbnb$_t$
p	6	5	6
	5	6	6
q_2	6	6	6
BOUNDS	3406.3***	6.26***	1.53
Π	− 0.87*** (0.006)	− 3.41*** (0.51)	− 0.87** (0.25)
β_1	− 1.066*** (0.19)	− 0.83*** (0.15)	− 0.94 (0.45)
β_2	− 0.90*** (0.20)	− 0.78** (0.20)	− 1.11* (0.45)
β_{trend}	0.016*** (0.003)	0.012** (0.004)	0.018 (0.014)
LM(2)	0.47 [0.68]	1.55 [0.39]	0.43 [0.73]
HETTEST	1.50 [0.38]	0.50 [0.88]	1.75 [0.36]

Legend: ***: significance at the 1%, **: at 5% level, and *: 10% level addition, the numbers in square brackets below the F-statistics for the serial correlation test show the relevant p-values for the tests.

Results and discussion

The results in Table 5.1 show that all three models are well specified regarding serially correlated error terms and heteroskedasticity. Co-integration is found, i.e., we reject the null hypothesis of no co-integration between the variables at the 1% significance level for Model 1 and at the 5% significance level for Model 2, but a long-run relationship – and thereby long-run causality – is not found in Model 3 according to the bounds test. The estimated coefficient on the error correction term Π is -0.87 for model 1, indicating that changes in the number of Airbnb rentals is a function of disequilibrium in the co-integrating relationship, i.e., the long run. This coefficient is -3.41 for model 2, such that number of traditional overnight stays over-reacts (since its absolute value is larger than unity) to disequilibrium in the co-integrating relationship. For Model 3, we have a significant long-run coefficient, but since the bounds test does not find co-integration, we do not interpret this as error correcting behaviour.

We also see from the long-run coefficients in Models 1 and 2 that all of these are significant and negative, indicating that the number of Airbnb rentals decreases if the number of traditional overnight stays increases or the unemployment rate increases. However, the number of overnight stays decreases if the number of Airbnb rentals increases or the unemployment rate increases. In particular, the long-run coefficients show that a one percent increase in numbers of Airbnb listings will decrease traditional accommodation by 0.83%, and a one percent increase in the unemployment rate will cause a 0.90% decrease in the number of Airbnb listings, ceteris paribus. Hence, higher unemployment has a negative effect on the number of Airbnb rentals, suggesting that there is no indication of necessity entrepreneurship, but rather opportunity entrepreneurship (Acs, 2006). The negative effect of the number of Airbnb rentals on traditional accommodation indicates "hotelization", which is in line with the definition given in Lee (2016) on this relationship. From Model 3, we see no co-integration, indicating that Airbnb rentals and overnight stays do not affect the unemployment rate in the long run; this result also shows that the development in tourism over the sample does not seem to have had an effect on regional economic development. Even though we see effects in the long run over the sample, the sample size and the number of variables used in this analysis are too small to draw this conclusion. Hence, future empirical research on the effects between Airbnb and regional economic development indicators could provide more results using larger data sets.

Conclusion and outlook

This book chapter defines the suppliers of short-term housing to the Airbnb-brokered accommodation market as digital entrepreneurs and looks into the link between such digital entrepreneurship and regional economic development. A regional case study in Norway, the southeastern county of Østfold, is used because it represents a secondary tourist destination in Norway. Based on a theoretical framework, we find that digital entrepreneurs associated with Airbnb are influenced by the prevalence of "traditional" accommodation and driven by unemployment in the region.

It gives rise to two findings: First, there is evidence that Airbnb's growth is linked to the unemployment rate in a region, with higher unemployment decreasing this growth. This finding suggests that digital entrepreneurship in the sharing economy using Airbnb is associated with opportunity entrepreneurship rather than necessity entrepreneurship. In fact, we do not find evidence in favour of necessity entrepreneurship with the empirical analysis presented even if the descriptive statistics might have suggested so based on the relatively high unemployment rate in Østfold. Second, Airbnb rentals seem to affect traditional accommodation negatively, indicating that the Airbnb is used as a substitute for this, in line with the theoretical definition of "hotelization" (Lee, 2016). This result also shows that digital entrepreneurs using Airbnb can influence tourism in a region by providing extra facilities alongside an existing accommodation sector. For secondary touristic regions with a limited number of "traditional" accommodation facilities, Airbnb-based entrepreneurs might not only respond to but also create extra demand for accommodation. This is contrary to the analysis in Strømmen-Bakhtiar and Vinogradov (2019) who found a positive effect from Airbnb on hotel nights sold. However, we only focus on the particular region of Østfold where Airbnb can be affected differently as it is a secondary touristic destination. In addition, we include other traditional accommodation services such as pensions and camping sites to our analysis.

Altogether, these preliminary findings highlight that digital entrepreneurs can contribute to regional economic development by making regions more attractive as a touristic destination (see the definition by Stimson et al., 2006, p. 6). Given the scarce evidence provided in this book chapter, the ideas collected here may open the door for future empirical research. First, as the limitation of this study, the empirical sample used for the analysis is short and does not include other variables than (un)employment and overnight stays as proxies for regional economic growth respectively the touristic potential in a region. Future research should look more closely into the causal relationships spotted here, refining the model with a broader set of indicators. Second, the specific relationship between Airbnb and the demand for touristic accommodation in a region remains blurry, and therefore, follow-up research might investigate this relationship in more detail. Finally, it should also be mentioned that the negative effects of Airbnb for big cities have been recently demonstrated (Kaplan & Nadler, 2015), and there are ongoing discussions among policy-makers about the regulation of Airbnb. With this chapter, we stress the ambiguity of the effects that digital entrepreneurs in the sharing economy might have with regard to regional economic development. This question is relevant, for example, with regard to the revitalisation of rural-peripheral areas as touristic destinations and the entrepreneurial opportunities for residents in such regions, which may generate a positive effect on regional economic development, versus other, potential negative effects.

Notes

1 The beginning of the sample may not include all actual listings, but we still observe a positive trend from October 2015 until the end of the sample.
2 According to Airdna.co, the number of active Airbnb and Homeaway rentals have grown from 4,248 in the first quarter of 2016 to 5,066 in the beginning in 2019, i.e., a growth of 19%.
3 Data for the number of Airbnb listings is from Airdna and data for overnight stays is from Statistics Norway. Data for the unemployment rate in Østfold is from the Norwegian Labour and Welfare Administration (NAV), and is not the same as in Figure 5.4 which only provides annual data for the unemployment rate in our sample. All of the data series are monthly.

References

Acs, Z. 2006. How Is Entrepreneurship Good for Economic Growth? *Innovations*, 1, 1, 97–107.

Acs, Z. & Armington, C. 2004. Employment Growth and Entrepreneurial Activity in Cities. *Regional Studies*, 38, 8, 911–927.

Acs, Z. J., Audretsch, D. B., Braunerhjelm, P. & Carlsson, B. 2012. Growth and Entrepreneurship. *Small Business Economics*, 39, 2, 289–300.

Angulo-Guerrero, M. J., Perez-Moreno, S. & Abad-Guerrero, S. M. 2017. How Economic Freedom Affects Opportunity and Necessity Entrepreneurship in the OECD Countries. *Journal of Business Research*, 73, 30–37.

Baumol, W. J. 2010. *The Microtheory of Innovative Entrepreneurship*. Princeton and Oxford: Princeton University Press.

Baumol, W. J. 1968. Entrepreneurship in Economic Theory. *The American Economic Review*, 58, 2, 64–71.

Bloomberg. 2018. *The Company Overview of Airbnb, Inc.*. Retrieved from web.archive.org/web/20180108004352/www.bloomberg.com/research/stocks/private/snapshot.asp?privcapId=115705393. on 27 April 2019.

Braunerhjelm, P., Acs, Z. J., Audretsch, D. B. & Carlsson, B. 2010. The Missing Link: Knowledge Diffusion and Entrepreneurship in Endogenous Growth. *Small Business Economics*, 32, 2, 105–125.

Carland, J. W., Hoy, F., Boulton, W. R. & Carland, J. A. C. 1984. Differentiating Entrepreneurs from Small Business Owners: A Conceptualization. *The Academy of Management Review*, 9, 2, 354–359.

Carree, M. A. & Thurik, A. R. 2003. The Impact of Entrepreneurship on Economic Growth. In: Acs, Z. J. & Audretsch, D.B. (eds.), *Handbook of Entrepreneurship Research*. New York: Springer, 557–594.

Cheng, M. 2016. Sharing Economy: A Review and Agenda for Future Research. *International Journal of Hospitality Management*, 57, 60–70.

Cheng, M. & Foley, C. 2018. The Sharing Economy and Digital Discrimination: The Case of Airbnb. *International Journal of Hospitality Management*, 70, 95–98.

Foodsharing. Retrieved from https://foodsharing.de/. on 4 November 2019.

Geissinger, A., Laurell, C., Sandström, C., Eriksson, K. & Nykvist, R. 2018. Digital Entrepreneurship and Field Conditions for Institutional Change–Investigating the Enabling Role of Cities. *Technological Forecasting and Social Change.* Online first.

Giacomin, O., Janssen, F., Guyot, J.-L. & Lohest, O. 2011. Opportunity And/or Necessity Entrepreneurship? The Impact of the Socio-Economic Characteristics of Entrepreneurs. MRPA Paper. München, University München.

Giones, F. & Brem, A. 2017. Digital Technology Entrepreneurship: A Definition and Research Agenda. *Technology Innovation Management Review*, 7, 5, 44–51.

Grèzes, V., Lehmann, B. G., Schnyder, M. & Perruchoud, A. 2016. A Process for Co-Creating Shared Value with the Crowd: Tourism Case Studies from A Regional Innovation System in Western Switzerland. *Technology Innovation Management Review*, 6, 11.

Grimes, S. 2003. The Digital Economy Challenge Facing Peripheral Rural Areas. *Progress in Human Geography*, 27, 2, 174–193.

Gyimóthy, S. & Meged, J. W. 2018. The Camøno: A Communitarian Walking Trail in the Sharing Economy. *Tourism Planning & Development*, 15, 5, 496–515.

Gössling, S. & Michael Hall, C. 2019. Sharing versus Collaborative Economy: How to Align ICT Developments and the SDGs in Tourism? *Journal of Sustainable Tourism*, 27, 1, 74–96.

Haefliger, S., Jäger, P. & Von Krogh, G. 2010. Under the Radar: Industry Entry by User Entrepreneurs. *Research Policy*, 39, 9, 1198–1213.

HomeExchange. Retrieved from https://www.homeexchange.com/ on 4 November 2019.

Hull, C. E., Caisy Hung, Y.-T., Hair, N., Perotti, V. & Demartino, R. 2007. Taking Advantage of Digital Opportunities: A Typology of Digital Entrepreneurship. *International Journal of Networking and Virtual Organisations*, 4, 3, 290–303.

Joshi, M. & Yermish, I. 2000. The Digital Economy: A Golden Opportunity for Entrepreneurs. *The Digital Economy*, 3, 1, 15–21.

Kaplan, R. A. & Nadler, M. L. 2015. Airbnb: A Case Study in Occupancy Regulation and Taxation. *University of Chicago Law Review Dialogue*, 82, 1, 103–115.

Kozinets, R. V., De Valck, K., Wojnicki, A. C. & Wilner, S. J. 2010. Networked Narratives: Understanding Word-of-Mouth Marketing in Online Communities. *Journal of Marketing*, 74, 2, 71–89.

Kraus, S., Palmer, C., Kailer, N., Kallinger, F. L. & Spitzer, J. 2019. Digital Entrepreneurship. *International Journal of Entrepreneurial Behavior & Research*, 25, 2, 353–375.

Lee, D. 2016. How Airbnb Short-Term Rentals Exacerbate Los Angeles's Affordable Housing Crisis: Analysis and Policy Recommendations. *Harvard Law & Policy Review*, 10, 229.

Liu, Y.-D. 2014. Cultural Events and Cultural Tourism Development: Lessons from the European Capitals of Culture. *European Planning Studies*, 22, 3, 498–514.

Malecki, E. J. 1993. Entrepreneurship in Regional and Local Development. *International Regional Science Review*, 16, 1–2, 119–153.

Ministry of Trade, Industry, and Fisheries. 2019. *Business and Industry in Norway – The Structure of the Norwegian Economy*. Retrieved from www.regjeringen.no/en/dokumenter/Business-and-industry-in-Norway—The-structure-of-the-Norwegian-economy/id419326/ on 20 June 2019.

Mosedale, J. & Voll, F. 2017. Social Innovations in Tourism: Social Practices Contributing to Social Development. In: Sheldon P. & Daniele R. (eds.), *Social Entrepreneurship and Tourism*. Cham: Tourism on the Verge. Springer, 101–115.

Mueller, P. 2007. Exploiting Entrepreneurial Opportunities: The Impact of Entrepreneurship on Growth. *Small Business Economics*, 28, 4, 355–362.

Narayan, P. K. & Smyth, R. 2005. Electricity Consumption, Employment and Real Income in Australia Evidence from Multivariate Granger Causality Tests. *Energy Policy*, 33, 9, 1109–1116.

North, D. & Smallbone, D. 2000. The Innovativeness and Growth of Rural SMEs during the 1990s. *Regional Studies*, 34, 2, 145–157.

OECD. 2018. *The Megaregion of Western Scandinavia*. Paris: Organisation for Economic Cooperation and Development.

Oner, A. & Kunday, O. 2016. A Study on Schumpeterian and Kirznerian Entrepreneurship in Turkey: 2006–2013. *Technological Forecasting and Social Change*, 102, 62–71.

Pedersen, E. R. G. & Netter, S. 2015. Collaborative Consumption: Business Model Opportunities and Barriers for Fashion Libraries. *Journal of Fashion Marketing and Management*, 19, 3, 258–273.

Pesaran, M. H. & Shin, Y. 1998. An Autoregressive Distributed-Lag Modelling Approach to Cointegration Analysis. *Econometric Society Monographs*, 31, 371–413.

Pesaran, M. H., Shin, Y. & Smith, R. J. 2001. Bounds Testing Approaches to the Analysis of Level Relationships. *Journal of Applied Econometrics*, 16, 3, 289–326.

Prieger, J. E., Bampoky, C., Blanco, L. R. & Liu, A. 2016. Economic Growth and the Optimal Level of Entrepreneurship. *World Development*, 82, 95–109.

Richter, C., Kraus, S., Brem, A., Durst, S. & Giselbrecht, C. 2017. Digital Entrepreneurship: Innovative Business Models for the Sharing Economy. *Creativity and Innovation Management*, 26, 3, 300–310.

Richter, C., Kraus, S. & Syrjä, P. 2015. The Shareconomy as a Precursor for Digital Entrepreneurship Business Models. *International Journal of Entrepreneurship and Small Business*, 25, 1, 18–25.

Sautet, F. 2013. Local and Systemic Entrepreneurship: Solving the Puzzle of Entrepreneurship and Economic Development. *Entrepreneurship Theory and Practice*, 37, 2, 387–402.

Schumpeter, J. 1911. *The Theory of Economic Development*. Cambridge: Harvard University Press.

Selstad, T. 2003. *Framtid for Østfold. Nye Scenarier 2020*. Lillehammer: Østlandsforskning.

Shane, S. & Venkataraman, S. 2000. The Promise of Entrepreneurship as a Field of Research. *Academy of Management Review*, 25, 1, 217–226.

Standing, C. & Mattsson, J. 2018. "fake It until You Make It": Business Model Conceptualization in Digital Entrepreneurship. *Journal of Strategic Marketing*, 26, 5, 385–399.

Statistics Norway (2019a). Table number 08401: Accommodation establishments total. Guest nights, by guests' country of residence. Retrieved from https://www.ssb.no/en/statbank/table/08401/ on 6 November 2019.

Statistics Norway (2019b). Table number 10593: Unemployed persons registered at the Employment Offices 15-74 years, by sex (per cent). Retrieved from https://www.ssb.no/en/statbank/table/10593/ on November 6 2019.

Sternberg, R. 2011. Regional Determinants of Entrepreneurial Activities - Theories and Empirical Evidence. In: Fritsch, M. (ed.), *Handbook of Research on Entrepreneurship and Regional Development. National and Regional Perspectives*. Cheltenham: Edward Elgar, 33–57.

Stimson, R. J., Stough, R. R. & Roberts, B. H. 2006. *Regional Economic Development: Analysis and Planning Strategy*. Heidelberg: Springer.

Strømmen-Bakhtiar, A. & Vinogradov, E. 2019. The Effects of Airbnb on Hotels in Norway. *Society and Economy*, 41, 1, 87–105.

Sussan, F. & Acs, Z. J. 2017. The Digital Entrepreneurial Ecosystem. *Small Business Economics*, 49, 1, 55–73.

Urbano, D. & Aparicio, S. 2016. Entrepreneurship Capital Types and Economic Growth: International Evidence. *Technological Forecasting and Social Change*, 102, 34–44.

Valliere, D. & Peterson, R. 2009. Entrepreneurship and Economic Growth: Evidence from Emerging and Developed Countries. *Entrepreneurship and Regional Development*, 21, 5–6, 459–480.

Van Stel, A., Carree, M. & Thurik, R. 2005. The Effect of Entrepreneurial Activity on National Economic Growth. *Small Business Economics*, 24, 3, 311–321.

Van Stel, A., Thurik, R., Stam, F. & Hartog, C. 2010. *Ambitious Entrepreneurship, High-Growth Firms and Macroeconomic Growth*. Zoetermeer: Panteia/EIM.

Weitzenboeck, E. M. 2015. Looking Back to See Ahead: The Changing Face of Users in European E-Commerce Law. *Artificial Intelligence and Law*, 23, 3, 201–215.

Wennekers, S. & Thurik, R. 1999. Linking Entreprepreneurship and Economic Growth. *Small Business Economics*, 13, 27–55.

Zervas, G., Proserpio, D. & Byers, J. W. 2017. The Rise of the Sharing Economy: Estimating the Impact of Airbnb on the Hotel Industry. *Journal of Marketing Research*, 54, 5, 687–705.

6 Sharing economy in Arctic offshore logistics

A paradigm shift in facilitating emergency preparedness

Antonina Tsvetkova

Introduction

Offshore maritime logistics operations are essential in the value chain between the supply base and the offshore drilling and production units to ensure continuous offshore activities. Resource strategies that allocate and manage a bundle of appropriate resources and distinct competencies are required to gain a high level of functionality and make offshore operations both economically and technically sustainable. However, within a supply chain and logistics operations, resource heterogeneity may occur due to their different capabilities and purpose of utilisation. It can engender situations in which the amount of productive and strategic resources is limited and scarce in relation to its demand (Peteraf, 1993). This, in turn, may result in shortfalls in resource utilisation and resource allocation along the supply chain without a desirable combination of resources to subsequently increase their efficiency.

In recent years, oil and gas companies have embraced the sharing economy principles primarily to cut costs. At the same time, sharing economy has generated innovative practices and logistics strategies like the allocation of the shared resource and the shared information. Thereby, the sharing initiatives have gained the potential to substantially affect established business models, and management approaches in a revolutionary way. However, there is a lack of research on how the sharing economy principles and collaborative utilisation of resources impact on offshore logistics operations.

Further, the literature on the sharing economy in a logistics context mostly concentrates on resources accessibility and flexibility of their utilisation related to the customer-to-customer (C2C) and business-to-customer (B2C) markets (Teubner, 2014). This type of sharing process has become a common practice for people today that is strongly supported by mobile phone applications and websites. Although the various sharing experiences like ride-sharing and, in particular, Uber in the B2C markets have gained significant attention in the literature and public debate, these initiatives of collaborative consumption in the business-to-business (B2B) market are still underexplored despite a lot of potentials. The B2B sharing economy imposes certain features on interactions between companies like external resource orchestration rather than controlling internal resources, as well as external interactions between companies instead of internal optimisation. However, there is still a lack of understanding of how the B2B sharing economy practice creates shared value and solve challenges related to liability issues between companies, in particular within offshore field projects.

It is worth noting that offshore logistics value has been recognised not only in cargo delivery but also in providing extra support regarding safety at sea, environmental considerations, and security standards according to international regulations (Kristiansen, 2005). Also, Borch and Batalden (2015) argue that due to the complexity of offshore operational issues, the offshore logistics systems should be constituted through the discovery and deployment of specific value-creating activities (Borch and Batalden, 2015). At the same time, the literature on offshore operations primarily concentrates on vessel routing issues with cargo deliveries and development of a coherent schedule for supply vessels between offshore installations and onshore facilities (Fagerholt and Lindstad, 2000; Aas et al., 2007; Halvorsen-Weare et al., 2012; Sopot and Gribkovskaya, 2014). Offshore supply operations and vessel routines are often studied in isolation from their adoption in real cases through the development of optimal routine models and scenarios. Without considering the influence of contextual factors on how offshore supply operations are deployed, their feasibility and resilience may become problematic, particularly about the use of supply vessels (Borch and Batalden, 2015). Thus, it seems like there is a lack of understanding of how collaborative utilisation of offshore resources can facilitate the development of offshore field projects in practice while promoting "shared value" processes.

Motivated by the above-mentioned shortcomings in the literature, the present study aims *to explore how the sharing economy principles emerge and influence offshore logistics operations by facilitating value-creating activities in response to contextual influence.*

In doing so, the study presents two empirical cases of resource sharing and collaborative utilisation within the development of offshore field projects in the Norwegian Barents Sea. Recently oil and gas companies have moved their offshore operations further north and into the remote Arctic areas. However, the Arctic Seas are characterised by numerous challenging conditions like severe natural conditions (low temperatures, icing, polar lows, darkness), remoteness from harbours and land infrastructure, and vulnerability of the ecosystem (Milaković et al., 2015). There is confusion in understanding about how the sharing economy can benefit in environments full of uncertainties and complexities like the Arctic ice-infested waters. Both cases illustrate collaborative utilisation of offshore resources in response to contextual challenges and regulations both oil companies face when developing their offshore field projects in the Norwegian Barents Sea.

The study is organised as follows: the next section presents a review of the leading research in the field of collaborative consumption and sharing economy, which highlights the research gap in the area of logistics. Then the research method is described. The following section presents two empirical cases defining offshore logistics operations at work in collaborative consumption. The theoretical and managerial implications are discussed then. The conclusion reviews the contribution of this study and proposes the agenda for future research.

Sharing economy and collaborative consumption in logistics

A central idea of the sharing economy is the optimisation of unused or under-used assets (physical assets or intangible assets) by pooling or sharing them through digital platforms (Benkler, 2004). Thus, the sharing economy either connect individuals or companies through platforms to carry out sales, rentals, swaps, or donations (Gansky, 2012) or establish more centralised "product-service systems" to provide access instead of use. The sharing economy has been recognised as a complex economic activity because it combines features from both market and non-market logics, including a variety of cognitive and normative frames that are encapsulated in very different types of organisations (Acquier et al., 2019).

Collaborative consumption or utilisation as part of the sharing economy emphasises the commercial aspects of sharing (Dreyer et al., 2017) and rather intensifies the use of idle assets (Botsman and Rogers, 2010). It is generally defined by characteristics like non-ownership, temporary access and redistribution of material goods or less tangible assets like money, space and time (Kathan et al., 2016). Further, it is denoted that individuals or companies prefer to pay for assets or services by consumption rather than owing assets permanently or making long-term contracts for services (Deloitte, 2016).

The literature on collaborative consumption or utilisation is not well developed, although this topic has widely publicised in plentiful popular literature like the press, blogs by associations and experts, open-access publications, etc. (Carbone et al., 2018). Several research streams have, however, emerged and highlighted ongoing debates in the literature. Several previous research have emphasised that collaborative consumption holds great promise in terms of sustainability by combining environmental concerns for resource optimisation, a social orientation towards communities and social exchange, and pointing to market opportunities (Lichtenthaler, 2016; Voytenko Palgan et al., 2017). It is also related to shared-value creation as it "involves creating economic value in a way that also creates value for society by addressing its needs and challenges" (Porter and Kramer, 2011). The concept of shared value can be determined as "policies and operating practices that enhance competitiveness of a company while simultaneously advancing the economic and social conditions in the communities in which it operates. [...] Value is defined as benefits relative to costs, not just benefits alone" (Porter and Kramer, 2011).

At the same time, some studies have shown that the environmental benefits of the sharing economy may be exaggerated because economic pursuit generally prevails over environmental concerns in users' motivations (Barnes and Mattsson,

2016; Böcker and Meelen, 2017). Further, the societal benefits may become possible in certain environments after the satisfaction of economic and environmental concerns (Tsvetkova, 2020a). It seems like there is a lack of understanding of how collaborative utilization of resources may contribute to value creation, value distribution and societal impacts (Acquier et al., 2017).

Method

Research design

The present empirical study draws on the case study research method. Two cases presented various offshore field projects located in the Norwegian Barents Sea. The two key dimensions to be considered for case selection were 1) experience in decision-making on reallocation and re-routing the transport resources in an optimal way when it is needed and 2) experience in integrating the sharing economy principles into offshore logistics operations. The sample included two stages of offshore operational management – exploitation with oil production and exploration – to illustrate the challenges for offshore operations and the potential influence of contextual factors on resource-allocation strategy implementation in different Arctic environments.

The case study method allowed an investigation to obtain the meaningful characteristics of real-life events and capture the contextual settings of the offshore field projects where the sharing economy principles emerged and were translated into offshore logistics practice. This research method was helpful to reveal the potential contextual influence on offshore logistics operations and to perceive how the sharing economy principles enabled to generate innovative solutions in implementing resource allocation strategies. The analysis of two cases allowed developing a more elaborated knowledge of the underlying mechanisms of the sharing economy that facilitate the deployment of value-creating activities and societal impacts within offshore logistics operations in the Norwegian Barents Sea. Both cases emphasised complementary aspects of the studied phenomenon.

Data collection

Qualitative data was collected from multiple sources, as recommended in previous logistics research (Voss et al., 2002). Fourteen semi-structured and in-depth face-to-face interviews and six telephone interviews were conducted with senior managers from several oil companies, operating in the Arctic Seas, shipping companies, vessel-designers, ice management consulting companies, international ice advisory boards. All the respondents were selected for their experience and practical knowledge in operating offshore field projects, supply logistics, ice management, and outsourcing decision-making processes.

The use of the semi-structured interview guide enabled asking additional questions by providing clarifications of particular issues or helping to keep the interview focus on the intended topics, especially when the respondents had difficulty in expressing their opinions and views. All the interviews (done by the first author) were tape-recorded with the consent of the respondents while making hand-written notes; transcribed, validated with the respondents, and consequently analysed. The interviews took place in Bergen, Oslo, Kristiansand and Tromsø (Norway) during two periods of June 2017 and August to October 2017. The interviews were conducted in English and Norwegian. The non-English interview answers were translated into English then. When necessary, follow-up interviews with additional questions were conducted via email, telephone or in-person. To comply with ethical issues, it was deemed necessary to omit the companies' and respondents' names.

Other data were collected from secondary sources such as companies' documentation, press releases, research reports within the project "Operational logistics and business process management in High Arctic oil & gas operations" (Oplog), as well as legislative laws and regulatory policies on offshore operations in Arctic Seas. The documentary sources helped in the preparation of interviewing and, later on, analysing the empirical data to complement the findings. Using several different types of data sources allowed us increasing the internal consistency of data and validity of research findings (Voss et al., 2002; Yin, 2009).

Data analysis

Each of the case stories started with the description of contextual settings, resource configuration, logistics process, and emergency preparedness system within the development of offshore operations. The collaborative utilisation of offshore resources was explored and proceeded to resource-allocation strategies perspectives to discover value-creating activities.

The case presentation was based on many qualitative pieces of data, including the individual perceptions and experiences of senior managers of the operators. Interview citations were used to support the claims made in the coherent description of resource-allocation strategy implementation within the offshore operations. The analysis included an iterative process of reading, coding, and interpretation of the transcribed personal interviews and observation notes (Hall and Nordqvist, 2008) of two cases. The iterative process allowed identifying patterns across both cases, as well as ensure consistency and improve inter-rater reliability (Pagell and Krause, 2005).

A cross-case analysis was conducted to move from the two specific cases to the identification of a general perception of how the sharing economy principles evolved in the Norwegian Barents Sea and facilitated value-creating activities through the implementation of resource-allocation strategies in the development of offshore field projects in response to contextual challenges. This helped in exploring what research elements might be replicable in different areas of the Norwegian Barents Sea (Miles and Huberman, 1994; Yin, 2009).

Offshore logistics operations in the Arctic environments: Context description

Offshore logistics systems primarily aim to supply offshore operations with all necessary cargoes and services (Milaković et al., 2015) regularly as planned and in a cost-efficient way (Aas et al., 2009; Fagerholt and Lindstad, 2000). So, the overall value of the offshore logistics system is maritime transportation of goods and services, which plays a bridging role between the offshore installations and the onshore supply base with the focus on optimisation and efficiency (Borch and Batalden, 2015). The focus on optimization and efficiency in the literature addresses vessel routing issues with cargo deliveries and resource configuration (Fagerholt and Lindstad, 2000; Sopot and Gribkovskaya, 2014) to achieve low cost and make relationships between offshore activities and onshore facilities more efficient and integrated (Medda and Trujillo, 2010; Borch and Batalden, 2015). However, previous research considers offshore operations in isolation from their adoption in real practice by building models and scenarios and, thereby, a common understanding of how contextual conditions affect the development of offshore operations is underexplored. Further, the possible volatility of contextual settings increases risks and makes it challenging to map cause-effect relations for decision-making and implementation of supply chain strategies (Kristiansen, 2005; Panayides, 2006; Tsvetkova and Gammelgaard, 2018).

The present study addresses the sharing economy principles in the development of offshore field projects in the Arctic seas. The Arctic provides challenging contextual settings, including remoteness and infrastructure limitations (with long distances between the supply base and offshore operations, lack of self-sufficiency and communication); cold climate and harsh weather conditions (with low temperatures, icing, high density fog and low speed of supply vessels); winter darkness and etc. (Borch, 2018). These settings make navigation and offshore operations challenging, impose limitations of logistics resources and demand on a particular design of supply vessels and specific equipment onboard.

Another maritime logistics value has been recognised in providing additional support concerning safety at sea and environmental considerations according to international regulations (Kristiansen, 2005). Due to the complexity of offshore operational issues, long distances from the shore and supply bases, as well as logistics challenges related to low temperatures and poor daylight conditions, emergency preparedness and oil response capability become a special and even rather essential functions for the development of offshore field projects in Arctic waters. The potential capability of logistics resources involved to take extra functions without increasing their amount and hence costs has been emphasised by the previous researchers (Borch and Kjerstad, 2018; Tsvetkova, 2020b). However, there is still a lack of knowledge of how the variability of resource allocation and preparedness to it within the offshore logistics system can facilitate value-creating activities, in particular providing emergency preparedness to oil spills and search-and-rescue (SAR) operations.

Case presentation

Case A. involvement of fishermen

Location and natural conditions

The offshore exploitation operations with oil production have taken place in the South-Western Norwegian sector of the Barents Sea, 88 kilometers northwest of the supply base, in water depths of 341m.

The weather conditions in this region cause challenges for offshore operations mostly in winter with the added probable danger of icing from sea spray in the cold. There are also cold winds from the south and in the winter, darkness and −30°C temperatures make working on the rig tough to endure. Sudden storms and hurricanes are also a possibility due to occasional deep troughs of low pressure. In these conditions, the equipment can break more often and in unpredictable ways, and repairs and maintenance can be a lengthier process.

Resource configuration and logistics process

The offshore operations were served by the following units: a floating, production, storage, and off-loading platform; two platform supply vessels "Stril Barents" and "Skandi Iceman" for supply and anchor handling duties; one emergency response and rescue vessel "Esvagt Aurora" for stand by duties and preparedness.

The logistics process was quite predictable, although the long distance from the supply base increased risks to ensure the development of offshore operations. The supply vessels were constantly on the move between the supply base and the offshore platform with a normal transit time of four hours that might increase in case of bad weather. As emphasised by a senior manager of the operator: "Due to weather conditions and unforeseen situations, there were frequent changes of plans and delays in cargo transport that caused frequent changes of orders and many stand by hours for new orders from the logistics coordinators".

Emergency preparedness

The logistics system of so high-risk projects as the development of offshore operations includes not only maritime cargo transportation but also emergency preparedness. There were a number of challenges to SAR and oil spill preparedness like the remoteness; limited infrastructure; long response time for resources from the Norwegian Sea and the North Sea; limited light conditions and icing during the winter season. To address these challenges, the operator used a set of integrated systems to detect and monitor immediate discharges from the field platform like satellites, planes and helicopters (equipped with synthetic aperture radars, side-looking airborne radars, infra-red detectors), installation (with radars, infrared inspections), sensors on the subsea templates, land-based installations (with high frequency radar systems). As emphasised by a senior manager of the operator:

> Our logistics department has to monitor, anticipate and adequately respond to any possible emergencies and learn consequences. Anticipation is the most challenging area for logistical planning. The task is to allocate the transportation resources like vessels and helicopters in an optimal way that makes it possible to foresee possible changes in case of an emergency. But it is very difficult to overview all the risks and decrease the number of unplanned ad-hoc solutions. So, the logistics system always has to be on the alert for emergencies.

Further, the supply vessels were equipped with extra systems of oil spill protection, infrared cameras and oil-detecting radars, as well as they had a spreading capacity. The emergency response and rescue vessel that was optimised to deal with cold weather conditions was equipped with oil-spill protection. Additionally, infrared technology was developed to see the oil spill in darkness. Sensors in mini-buoys monitored the direction of an oil slick.

However, these innovative practices in SAR and oil spill response, triggered by the development of offshore operations in the cold conditions, were not enough. Despite the remote location of offshore operations from the coast, the hydrometeorological conditions like sea current and wind made the drifting time in case of any oil spill accident too short to reach the coastline in a matter of hours. That caused a challenge for developing contingency plans and managing emergency response systems in an efficient way in this area. As told by a senior manager of the operator:

> We decided to launch an integrated field oil spill detection and surveillance system mostly through implementing the permanent use of fishing vessels as a special acute phase task force. Our company as the operator together with the Fishermen's Association in Northern Norway and the Norwegian Coastal Administration established cooperation projects with the fisheries organizations and built a new permanent contingency organization, in which fishing vessels have contributed to oil recovery operations. This experience became one of the most significant innovations for the emergency preparedness system in Northern Norway.

The fishermen maintained their normal fishing practices, while their contribution to emergency preparedness came as an extra activity. This included regular courses, exercises, and potential real action. The fishermen were obliged to maintain their vessels in prescribed necessary conditions and to have the necessary equipment on board. Specific tasks of fishermen were to drag oil booms with their vessels to the emergency location, to monitor oil slicks, and to block off coastal inlets. They also had to report their accessibility and location. As emphasised a senior manager of the operator:

The partnership with fishermen was in favor because fishermen possess day-to-day current knowledge about sea currents, the influence of weather, waves, wind, and local geography. Another large advantage of the incorporation of local fishing boats is that they can be mobilised within a short time frame. Further, fishing boats can operate light and mid-weight boom systems.

There has always been a confrontation of interests between the petroleum industry and fisheries activity. The organization of oil spill response in the northern Norwegian waters showed an area where fisheries and oil companies have found common ground and the conflict has been less polarised. As told by a senior manager of the operator:

> The involvement of fishermen with relatively small vessels to be used in oil spill contingency operations demanded to extend the existing regulatory framework. Then, we could formally contract fishermen. This form of cooperation became a new kind of value creation for fisheries and the regional economy in the north. Now fishermen get a general financial reimbursement and specific compensations for days spent on training, courses, or real action. It is worth noting that the fishing vessels exercise at least twice a year. So, it is promising cooperation with mutual benefits for both industries that allowed us to increase emergency response actions along the coastline. Fishermen have demonstrated their high interest in participating in preparedness systems: when we just announced this opportunity, owners of more than 140 fishing vessels registered in the coastal response.

In the first instance, 30 local fishing vessels became a part of the emergency preparedness organization of the Norwegian continental shelf and started assisting during possible emissions that can reach coastal areas. The vessels were adapted and equipped with newly developed oil collection equipment that could be operated by a single fishing vessel and at higher speeds than the traditional system of lenses drawn by two vessels.

To increase coherence and test the field contingency equipment, the operator conducted several exercises in SAR and oil spill response near the offshore operations that allowed verifying the effectiveness and functionality of contingency plans.

Case B. collaborative utilization

Location and natural conditions

The offshore exploration (drilling) operations took place in the Northwestern part of the Barents Sea, at a distance of 415 km from the Norwegian coast. The water depth was 253 m. The drilling operations were fulfilled during four weeks.

The weather conditions in this region are similar to those in Case A. There is a relatively high probability of fog during summers and falls. The wave height can reach up to 13 m. In winter the location is characterised by low -30°C temperatures, heavy snowfalls, icing and occurrence of sea ice and icebergs that may cause challenges for offshore operations and equipment.

Resource configuration and logistics process

The offshore operations were served by the following units: a floating, self-propelled rig designed specifically for cold climates; two platform supply vessels "Troms Arcturus" and "Viking Queen" for supply and anchor handling duties; one emergency response and rescue vessel "Havila Troll" for stand by duties and preparedness.

The logistics process was quite predictable because the drilling operations were fulfilled during a very short favorable weather window. The long distance between the drilling site and the supply base (570 km) was one of the main challenges for planning logistics operations and ensuring regular support. It required 24 hours sailing per one way and two supply vessels made two round trips between the rig and the supply base.

Drilling operations are time-limited operations that should be completed during a very short period of time before the weather conditions change. Due to this, the supply vessels were constantly on the move between the bases and the drilling site in a given pattern. However, many delays caused by inefficient base handling and reduced visibility (mostly due to frequent fogs).

The rig crew was transported and changed by the helicopter with the flight time 1 hour 42 min. The crew shift was in two weeks. As told by a senior manager of the operator:

> Due to long distances and requirements on emergency preparedness, we could take on board the helicopter only seven passengers as the maximum at each flight because we needed capacity for extra fuel for the helicopter to reach the rig and back the shore base. So, if the crew onboard the rig was 120 persons, we changed 60 persons per week. It was risky to use the helicopter for the crew change for such long distances. Our logistics department had to anticipate cases when it was impossible to use helicopters. Then, supply vessels became an optimal solution for transporting personnel on time and be able to reallocate maritime resources in an optimal way not causing the delay in the offshore operations.

Emergency preparedness

The main challenges were remoteness from the shore, the abundance of fogs and limited infrastructure. To address these challenges, the operator had to take additional measures to upgrade its emergency preparedness during the exploration campaign. This involves the use of standby vessels with towing capacity, supply vessels, man overboard rescue boats, a hospital, infrared cameras and oil detecting radar systems, oil slick, a SAR helicopter, as well as a helipad on the rig. As emphasised by a senior manager:

It required too long preparations and many efforts to elaborate the logistics and emergency preparedness systems for so remote location from the shore – about eight months before the drilling operations started. We conducted some research to organize an optimal utilization of the logistical resources. However, some nuances might occur only during the project implementation.

The conditions of poor visibility due to frequent fogs in summers and falls and darkness in winters imposed restrictions on some methods of mapping and monitoring oil spills during any possible accidents and hence the effectiveness of operations. As told by a senior manager:

We had to monitor the current situation around the drilling operations and anticipate any possible changes that were likely to occur. That meant that we needed to be able to reallocate the logistical resources in an appropriate way if something went wrong. It was really stressful for managers to be constantly on the alert and predict risks that might cause accidents during the drilling campaign.

Oil spill recovery operations are about platforms for using skimmers for collecting oil, facilities for receiving and tank capacities for storing it, running oil booms, and dispersant capacity. As told by a senior manager:

Most of the supply vessels do not have the capacity onboard, but have to go shore, unload proceed to a depot, load the equipment and then transit to the site for oil recovery. This takes a lot of time both for making the equipment ready at base: transportation within 11 hours from the supply base, and make it ready on the site minimum within 2 hours. Generally, the recovery system is required to be in the sea within 5 hours, including alarm system, pumps, the standby vessel. However, in the Barents Sea, the recovery system should be in the sea within 2 hours for response in defined situations of hazards or accidents.

The analysis showed that there was no possibility for oil spills to reach the main coastline due to the remoteness with the exception of the nearby islands. But the expected potential dispersion of oil on the ocean was estimated about 120 km. The standby vessel being on duty close to the rig during 24 hours was equipped with oil spill protection equipment in compliance with the standards. In case of any possible accident, the vessel would be capable of commencing damage-limiting operations immediately within two hours, in the form of the deployment of marine booms and skimmer equipment. Further, according to the recommendations for so remote parts of the Arctic, the first supply vessel should be near the rig within 13 hours and the second supply vessel should be within 30 hours.

The remoteness undermined the availability and efficiency of the emergency preparedness system in case of an oil spill mostly due to the lack of resources, long time of resource reallocation and limited infrastructure. It required an extra capacity. Then, the operator elaborated an innovative solution to hire standby vessel "Esvagt Aurora" served at the same time for the offshore operations located at a distance of 293 nm and presented in Case A. The response time for this stand-by vessel was defined 26 hours to reach the drilling rig and commence damage-limiting operations. As emphasised by a senior logistician: "This shared standby vessel took part in the organised emergency exercise but it was assumed to support only in case of any possible emergency. This solution allowed strengthening the emergency preparedness in so remote area".

Further, SAR capacities are critical due to so long distance from the coastline and especially as the capacity of the All-Weather SAR (AWSAR) helicopters are stretched. The SAR capacities are about the pickup capacities of persons from the sea, including the number and size of man over board boats, fast going covered daughter crafts and persons one may accommodate onboard and hospital capacity. As told by a senior manager: "The offshore drilling operations were mostly in high waves. It was an important issue for the safe rescue of lifeboats and man over board boats in these conditions".

During the drilling operations, the operator shared two helicopters – a SAR helicopter and a transport helicopter – involved also in the offshore operations on the other site in the Barents Sea and presented in Case A. The shared transport helicopter could be also used as a SAR helicopter when needed. Both helicopters were equipped with the newly developed night vision technology that significantly improved SAR capacity in the darkness. As emphasised by a senior logistician:

> Maintaining an effective emergency response capability is critical to any organization contracting for helicopter operations in a hostile environment. The sharing utilization of both helicopters enhanced the capacity and flexibility of SAR operations, as well as long-term planning for the supplier. It was the first and positive experience of sharing two helicopters and the standby vessel served for another offshore project in case of any possible accidents and regular emergency exercises. We are going to share these helicopters again for developing the next offshore field next year.

However, near-site exercises revealed some shortcomings and risks when sharing strategically important and sought-after resources. In case of several emergencies in different locations at once, it can reveal serious obstacles for re-allocating sharing resources between two offshore sites at the same time for carrying out damage-limiting and SAR operations in an appropriate way.

Summary

The two cases illustrated that the sharing economy principles emerged in the Norwegian Barents Sea as a consequence of several contextual challenges that became critical for the development of offshore field projects in this area. These principles were incorporated as innovative solutions for resource sharing in implementing resource allocation strategies (see Table 6.1).

Discussion

The two cases illuminate how contextual challenges, primarily related to the remoteness from the onshore infrastructure and too long response time for extra resources, impose limitations on the offshore operational and logistics management. The integration and allocation of maritime resources based on various needs of offshore operations to make them effective and resilient determine the capacity of these resources to provide not only a regular connection between the supply base and the installations but also a support to emergency preparedness. The findings reveal a number of innovative solutions in sharing offshore resources in the Norwegian Barents Sea in response to the contextual challenges and logistics issues in order to be on the alert for any possible emergencies.

Although the theoretical and practical focus of the sharing economy is primarily the intensification of the use of idle assets and cost reduction, this study shows there are more sides to this process. The experience to involve fishermen with relatively small vessels, presented in Case A, enhanced the effectiveness and functionality of contingency plans in case of any possible emergencies rather than pursuing cost reduction issues. That allowed ensuring environmental safety in a more effective way.

In Case B, sharing of one stand by vessel and two helicopters concerned collaborative utilization of resources that are particularly in demand in offshore operations and were simultaneously involved in the other project rather than the use of idle or under-utilised assets. This new offshore practice of collaborative utilization in the Norwegian Barents Sea increased the capacity of emergency preparedness to SAR and oil spill response, improved flexibility in reallocating the logistical resources in case of accidents, as well as facilitated the feasibility of the offshore operations.

Sharing economy is not just a concept that can be plucked from the theoretical shelf and adapted anywhere and at any time. Contextual circumstances like climate, culture, regulation should be taken into consideration when employing the sharing economy principles; and the existing supply chain practices and resource allocation strategies should be prepared for changes.

Table 6.1 Transport resource sharing in the Norwegian Barents Sea

	Resource sharing emergence	Innovative solutions of resource sharing	Consequences
Case A	Contextual challenges: 1. To logistics: remoteness; lack of infrastructure; wind, storms, fogs, icing, polar nights. 2. To SAR and oil-spill Response- Closeness to the coast due to very short drifting time, long response time for resources from other locations, poor visibility due to polar nights.	Involvement of fishermen: - Fishermens' awareness about sea currents, influence of weather, waves, wind and local geography. - Fishing boats can be mobilised within a short time frame and can operate light and mind weight boom systems.	- Innovative practices in SAR and oil spill response. - Enhancing effectiveness and functionality of contingency plans. - Creating shared value for two confronting industries and society by ensuring environmental safety.
Case B	Contextual challenges: 1. To logistics: remoteness: lack of offshore resources;wind, storms, fogs, icing, polar nights. 2. To SAR and oil-spill Response: long Response time for resources from other locations, poor visibility due to frequent fogs and polar nights.	Offshore resource sharing: - A stand-by vessel from other projects to enhance damage– limiting operations in case of oil spills within 26 hours. - Two helicopters to improve SAR capacity, especially in the darkness and high waves.	- Creating shared value through ensuring the feasibility of offshore project development and environmental safety. - More flexibility in relocating the logistical resource in case of accidents. - Ensuring a special capacity for emergency preparedness for away from the onshore facilities.

Some previous research has praised the sharing economy for being a sustainable alternative to the current unsustainable economy for the promises of greater circulation of goods, the use of idle resources and more responsible consumption (Heinrichs, 2013; Voytenko Palgan et al., 2017). This study, however, demonstrates how the sharing economy contributes to the involvement of more resources that are in-demand in the market to enhance emergency preparedness and ensure environmental safety. The cases present the increase of the offshore projects' capacity to resist the influence of contextual challenges and was caused by the pursuit of the offshore projects need to be more feasible and resilient.

After evoking a number of changes in the existing practice of offshore operations in the Norwegian Barents Sea, the sharing economy principles facilitated not only value-creating activities like the emergency preparedness and environmental safety but also created shared value for society by addressing its needs and issues. The findings reveal that the innovative solution to use local fishing vessels in Case A has encouraged reconciliation of two confronting industries – petroleum versus fisheries activity – for creating shared value for both industries and society. So, the sharing economy logistics in the Norwegian Barents Sea increased the social responsibility of fishermen by imposing duties like monitoring oil slicks and dragging oil booms with their vessels to the emergency location but providing financial reimbursement and specific compensations for days spent on training or real action. High interest of fishermen without external regulation pressure to be involved was unexpected but allowed developing a community of committed participants in the emergency preparedness system to promote environmental and social values.

Although some previous research has shown that the environmental benefits may be overstated of the sharing economy (Barnes and Mattson, 2016; Böcker and Meelen, 2017). This study, however, shows that transport resource sharing in the Norwegian Barents Sea manifested itself as a value-driven strategy by enlightening the link between economic aspects, environmental and social issues. Thus, the knowledge of how the sharing economy principles emerge under the contextual challenges and constraints may change the existing offshore logistics practice and then create shared value for both confronting industries and society after their implementation contributes to a new understanding of sharing economy in the implementation of resource allocation strategies.

Conclusion and future research opportunities

The study presents the investigation of how the sharing economy principles emerge and influence offshore logistics operations in the Norwegian Barents Sea. It is further shown that some sharing economy principles can have some benefits and some trade-offs for reallocation of transport resources in an optimal way to be able to respond quickly to any possible emergencies in environments full of uncertainties and complexities like the Arctic demanding waters.

The extant literature on sharing economy in supply chain and logistics practices concentrates on information sharing issues. The analysis of both cases provides an understanding of how the sharing economy principles enable several value-creating activities of offshore logistics and create a shared value of collaborative resource utilisation for society and other local industries. Thus, this study contributes to theory by providing some empirical evidence of how the sharing economy logistics promote B2B collaboration in practice. Two cases presented in this study might be insufficient to confirm an emerging nature of the sharing economy and its influence on the sustainable development of offshore operations in Arctic waters. Therefore, more research should include case studies on sharing in supply chain management with regards to projects developing in different sectors and locations, including other alternative influences and factors. More research is needed to explore and potentially refine the approach of creating shared value suggested by Porter and Kramer (2011). There are still underestimated issues that future research needs to address how the sharing economy principles contribute to value-creating activities and how shared value is created for different participants involved.

References

Aas, B., Gribkovskaia, I. and Halskau, Ø. (2007). "Routing of supply vessels to petroleum installations", *International Journal of Physical Distribution & Logistics Management*, Vol. 37, No. 2, pp. 164–179.

Aas, B., Halskau, Ø. and Wallace, S.W. (2009). "The role of supply vessels in offshore logistics", *Maritime Economics & Logistics*, Vol. 11, No. Issue 3, pp. 302–325.

Acquier, A., Carbone, V. and Massé, D. (2019). "How to create value(s) in the sharing economy: business models, scalability, and sustainability", *Technology Innovation Management Review*, Vol. 9, No. 2, pp. 5–24.

Acquier, A., Daudigeos, T. and Pinkse, J. (2017). "Promises and paradoxes of the sharing economy: an organizing framework", *Technological Forecasting and Social Change*, Vol. 125, pp. 1–10.

Barnes, S.J. and Mattsson, J. (2016). "Understanding current and future issues in collaborative consumption: a four-stage Delphi study", *Technological Forecasting and Social Change*, Vol. 104, pp. 200–211.

Benkler, Y. (2004). "Sharing nicely: on shareable goods and the emergence of sharing as a modality of economic production", *The Yale Law Journal*, Vol. 114, No. 2, pp. 273–358.

Böcker, L. and Meelen, T. (2017). "Sharing for people, planet or profit? Analysing motivations for intended sharing economy participation", *Environmental Innovation and Societal Transitions*, Vol. 23, pp. 28–39.

Borch, O.J. (2018), "Offshore service vessels in high Arctic oil and gas field logistics operations – fleet configuration and the functional demands of cargo supply and emergency response vessels", *R&D Report #22*, Nord University.

Borch, O.J. and Batalden, B.-M. (2015). "Business-process management in high-turbulence environments: the case of the offshore service vessel industry", *Maritime Policy & Management*, Vol. 42, No. 5, pp. 481–498.

Borch, O.J. and Kjerstad, N. (2018). "The offshore oil and gas operations in ice infested water: resource configuration and operational process management", *Maritime Policy & Management*, Vol. 42, No. 5, pp. 481–498.

Botsman, R. and Rogers, R. (2010). *What's Mine Is Yours: How Collaborative Consumption Is Changing the Way We Live*. London: Collins.

Carbone, V., Rouquet, A. and Roussat, C. (2018). "A typology of logistics at work in collaborative consumption", *International Physical Distribution & Logistics Management*, Vol. 48, No. 6, pp. 570–585.

Deloitte (2016). The rise of the sharing economy. Impact on the transportation space, pp. 1–12.

Dreyer, B., Lüdeke-Freund, F., Hamann, R. and Faccer, K. (2017). "Upsides and downsides of the sharing economy: collaborative consumption business models' stakeholder value impacts and their relationship to context", *Technological Forecasting and Social Change*, Vol. 4, No. 6, pp. 2321–8916.

Fagerholt, K. and Lindstad, H. (2000). "Optimal policies for maintaining a supply service in the Norwegian Sea", *Omega*, Vol. 28, No. 3, pp. 269–275.

Gansky, L. (2012). *The Mesh: Why the Future of Business Is Sharing*. New York: Portfolio.

Hall, A. and Nordqvist, M. (2008). "Professional management in family businesses: toward an extended understanding", *Family Business Review*, Vol. 21, No. 1, pp. 51–65.

Halvorsen-Weare, E.E., Fagerholt, K., Nonås, L.M. and Asbjørnslett, B.E. (2012). "Optimal fleet composition and periodic routing of offshore supply vessels", *European Journal of Operational Research*, Vol. 223, pp. 508–517.

Heinrichs, H. (2013). "Sharing economy: a potential new pathway to sustainability", *GAIA – Ecological Perspectives for Science and Society*, Vol. 22, No. 4, pp. 228–231.

Kathan, W., Matzler, K. and Veider, V. (2016). "The sharing economy: your business model's friend or foe?", *Business Horizons*, Vol. 59, pp. 663–672.

Kristiansen, S. (2005). *Maritime Transport, Safety Management and Risk Analysis*. Burlington: Elsevier Butterworth-Heinemann.

Lichtenthaler, U. (2016). "Six principles for shared management: a framework for the integrated economy", *Journal off Business Strategy*, Vol. 37, No. 4, pp. 3–11.

Medda, F. and Trujillo, L. (2010). "Short-sea shipping: an analysis of its determinants", *Maritime Policy & Management*, Vol. 37, No. 3, pp. 285–303.

Milaković, A.-S., Ehlers, S., Westvik, M.H. and Schütz, P. (2015). "Offshore upstream logistics for operations in Arctic environment", in Ehlers, S., Asbjornslett, B.E., Rodseth, O.J. and Berg, T.E. (Eds.), *Maritime-Port Technology and Development*, Chapter 20, London, CRC Press 2014, pp. 163–170.

Miles, M.B. and Huberman, M.A. (1994). *Qualitative Data Analysis: An Expanded Sourcebook*. Thousand Oaks, CA: Sage.

Pagell, M. and Krause, D.R. (2005). "Determining when multiple respondents are needed in supply chain management research: the case of purchasing and operations", *Academy of Management Proceedings*, Vol. 2005, No.1, pp. 5–10.

Panayides, P.M. (2006). "Maritime policy, management and research: role and potential", *Maritime Policy & Management*, Vol. 33, No. 2, pp. 95–105.

Peteraf, M.A. (1993). "The cornerstones of competitive advantage: a resource based view", *Strategic Management Journal*, Vol. 14, No. 3, pp. 179–191.

Porter, M.E. and Kramer, M.R. (2011). "Creating shared value", *Harvard Business Review*, Vol. 89, No. 1/2, pp. 62–77.

Sopot, E. and Gribkovskaya, I. (2014). "Routing of supply vessels to with deliveries and pickups of multiple commodities", *Procedia Computer Science*, Vol. 31, pp. 910–917.

Teubner, T. (2014), "Thoughts on the sharing economy", International Conferences ICT 2014, pp. 322–326.

Tsvetkova, A. (2020a). "Social responsibility practice of the evolving nature in the sustainable development of Arctic maritime operations", in Pongrácz, E., Pavlov, V. and Hänninen, N. (Eds.), *In Search of Arctic Marine Sustainability: Arctic Maritime Businesses and the Resilience of the Marine Environment*, Heidelberg, Germany, Springer Polar Sciences, Springer, Chp. 6, in print.

Tsvetkova, A. (2020b). "The role of supply vessels in the development of offshore field projects in Arctic waters", in Pongrácz, E., Pavlov, V. and Hänninen, N. (Eds.), *In Search of Arctic Marine Sustainability: Arctic Maritime Businesses and the Resilience of the Marine Environment*, Heidelberg, Germany, Springer Polar Sciences, Springer, Chp. 12, in print.

Tsvetkova, A. and Gammelgaard, B. (2018). "The idea of transport independence in the Russian Arctic: a Scandinavian institutional approach to understanding supply chain strategy", *International Journal of Physical Distribution & Logistics Management*, Vol. 48, No. 9, pp. 913–930.

Voss, C., Tsikriktsis, N. and Frohlich, M. (2002). "Case research in operations management", *International Journal of Operations & Production Management*, Vol. 22, No. 2, pp. 195–219.

Voytenko Palgan, Y., Zvolska, L. and Mont, O. (2017). "Sustainability framings of accommodation sharing", *Environmental Innovation and Societal Transitions*, Vol. 23, pp. 70–83.

Yin, R.K. (2009). *Case Study Research: Design and Methods*. Thousand Oaks, CA: Sage.

Index

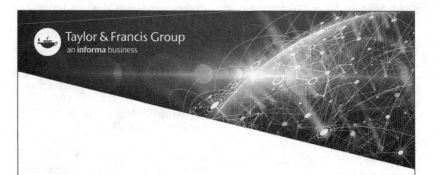

Printed in the United States
by Baker & Taylor Publisher Services